A HANDBOOK OF
DREAMS AND
FORTUNE-TELLING

JOSEPH INTERPRETING PHARAOH'S DREAM.

A HANDBOOK OF
DREAMS AND
FORTUNE-TELLING

Zadkiel and Sibly

SENATE

A Handbook of Dreams and Fortune-Telling

First published by W. Nicholson & Sons Ltd, London

This edition published in 1994 by Senate, an imprint of
Studio Editions Ltd, Princess House, 50 Eastcastle Street,
London W1N 7AP, England

ISBN 1 85958 056 4
Printed and bound in Guernsey by The Guernsey Press Co Ltd

DREAMS
AND THEIR INTERPRETATIONS.

ABANDON.—To dream that you abandon a person, is unfavourable; it intimates that you will lose friendships and favours which it will be very difficult to recover.—To dream that you are abandoned, denotes coming trouble.

ABBEY.—This denotes future comfort, peace of mind, freedom from anxiety.

ABDICATE.—To dream of a monarch abdicating his throne in any kingdom denotes anarchy and revolution there.

ABHOR.—To dream you are abhorred, not liked, and if you are troubled at the same, some enemies will injure you; if in your dream you are not troubled thereby, but rather defiant, it is a sign that you will surmount all opposition, and triumph over all your foes.

ABJECT.—Dreaming that you are in a forlorn and abject state, I fear, indicates coming poverty; if, in your dream, you appear cheerful under it, it will only be for a season, and prosperity will succeed.

ABORTION.—If a male dreams of this, trouble is approaching the partner of his life. If a female dreams of this, it is a dream of *caution;* beware; guard your health, or a sad calamity will ensue.

ABROAD.—To dream of being abroad, in a foreign country, denotes a change in your situation in life; you are likely to be unsettled in life, and to change your locality.

ABSCOND.—To dream that you abscond, or run away, is a sign that you are in danger of acting dishonourably; therefore, beware. If you dream of another person absconding; you will meet with a treacherous person—an unfaithful friend. Therefore, be on the look out. For a female to dream that her lover has absconded, is a sure sign that another possesses her heart, and vice versa.

ABSENT FRIENDS.—To dream of absent friends and that they are alive, but ill, indicates hasty intelligence, of a disagreeable nature; to dream that they are well denotes they are in a prosperous state, and that their friendship to you abides; to dream of the death of some absent friend foretells good news relating to a wedding.

ABSTAIN.—To dream that you are a total abstainer, denotes good health, success in life; great prosperity.

ABUNDANCE.—Dreaming of abundance denotes success in your plans, and a pleasing competence in life in consequence.

ABUSE.—To dream that some one is abusing you is a sure sign that you will quarrel with your lover, or your friend, and that some one has been speaking ill of you. In trade it indicates a great loss and often a robbery, therefore take care of your money. It would be as well also to be careful, when you retire to rest, of your fires and lights, as it often indicates loss of life and property by fire.

ABUSE.—To dream that you are abused and insulted, denotes that a dispute will arise between you and some one with whom you do business. If you are in love, be sure that some one has attempted to injure you with the object of your love, and is likely to succeed. Take heed, and be not slack in your attentions to your lover.

ABYSS.—Trouble, trouble is coming. You will be in straits and difficulties most formidable and from which it will be difficult for your friends to extricate you.

ACADEMY.—To dream that you are master, or mistress of an academy, indicates that you will be reduced in your circumstances; if single, that your intended marriage will be characterized by adversity.

ACCIDENT.—Dreaming that you meet with an accident to the injury of any part of your body, denotes coming personal affliction; but from which you will recover. To dream of an accident at sea, you will be crossed in love.

ACCUSE.—To dream that you are accused of a crime of which you are guilty, is a sign of great trouble, to dream that you are not found guilty, it denotes the failure of your enemy's evil designs, and that you will rise superior to all evil machinations. It denotes that you will acquire riches, by your own personal efforts, aided by the gifts of your friends.

ACHE.—To dream that you have aches and pains, denote a temporary illness, and some slight troubles.

ACORNS.—When you dream of acorns, it is a good sign; it betokens health, strength, and worldly abundance; if single, you are likely to marry well, and have a numerous and agreeable family. To a married woman it denotes the birth of twins. To tradesmen it is the omen of prosperity and wealth; and to all it is a good sign. To the lover it denotes success and happiness. To those in difficulties, a speedy deliverance.

ACQUAINTANCE.—To dream of an acquaintance, denotes his or their continued friendship. It is a sign that they are sincere.

ACQUIT.—To dream that you are charged with offence before a tribunal, and acquitted for want of evidence, is a sure sign of the utter confusion of your enemies, and of your own prosperity and stability.

ADMIRE.—To dream that you admire a person is an omen that your partner loves you, without ostentation; and if single, that your lover is sincere. To dream that you are admired betokens numerous friends.

ADULTERY.—Dreaming of being tempted to commit this crime, and of a successful resistance of it, intimates that in future life virtue will be your guide, and that you will greatly prosper; that your schemes and plans admirably succeed. But if you dream of being guilty of the vice, it is a sad omen of approaching troubles; that your prospects in love will be blasted, while despair will wring your heart with anguish.

ADVANCEMENT.—If you dream that you are advanced in your situation, it is a sign of success in all you undertake; if you are single, that your lover will be sincerely devoted to you. Altogether it is a favourable sign. If engaged in a law-suit, or any dispute, it is a sign that you will win.

ADVERSARY.—To dream you meet with an adversary, denotes that you will overcome some obstacle to your happiness; it denotes that your affairs will prosper, though you have enemies. If soliciting a situation, you will meet with impediments, yet you will overcome them.

ADVERSITY.—To dream of being in adverse circumstances is always a favourable dream ; It generally indicates the reverse, prosperity.

"Content and happy may they be
Who dream of cold adversity ;
To married man and married wife
It promises a happy life,
With many children, many friends ;
While unto others it portends
Success in love, success in trade,
A husband to the blooming maid
The farmer may expect each field
A full abundant crop to yield ;
The hardy sailor is sure to find
On his next voyage a favouring wind
And all will surely happy be
Who dream of cold adversity."

ADVICE.—To dream that you are receiving advice, denotes difficulties ; but you will have wise and faithful friends to help you. To dream that you are giving advice, is a sign that you will be highly esteemed by your friends and acquaintances.

ADVOCATE.—To dream that you are an advocate, or that you are advocating the cause of some one, is a sign that your future station will be a prominent one, and that for benevolent purposes, which will crown you with high honour, and gain you universal respect.

AFFILIATION.—To dream that you have a child fathered on you is a very bad dream, it indicates dreadful enemies, and a long and severe illness or else a sudden death. If you are about to make a journey by land or a voyage by sea, abandon it for some time to come, for

it will prove an unfortunate one to you; such a dream •
always foretells the loss of life or limb. For a young
woman to dream that she is fathering a child on some
one, implies that her life is actuated by improper
motives, and if he cannot secure his object he will
abandon her.

AFFLICTION.—It denotes a change of residence; to
the young and single early marriage, but not agreeable. It is not a good omen. It indicates trouble.

AFFLUENCE.—To dream of affluence is not very
favourable. It has frequently been found to denote
the contrary.

AFFRONT.—To dream that you are affronted by a
person denotes disappointment in love, and trouble
and vexation through one that owes you money; in
every case you will find it the forerunner of annoyance and discontent.

AFRAID.—This goes by the contrary. It denotes
that in future trials you will be valiant, and not afraid.
That your cause will succeed. That your lover will
prove true.

AGE.—A dream about your age betokens sickness,
and premature death.

AGUE.—To dream that you have the ague denotes
constant changes in your business and circumstances.
They will alternate; sometimes you will be prosperous, then poor. To dream that you and your lover
have both the ague, prognosticates that the connection
will be dissolved.

ALEHOUSE.—If you dream you are in an alehouse,
it denotes that you will be exposed to the malice of
low mean enemies. If a female dreams she is in an

alehouse, it is a sign that her future husband will love his cups. To dream that you are drinking ale with companions, denotes deception by the flatterer.

ALIEN.—To dream that you are an alien, or alienated, is a dream of contrary — the reverse will take place ; abiding friendship and love.

ALLIGATOR.—This denotes a sly crafty enemy ; and such a dream should excite to caution.

ALMONDS.—To dream of eating sweet almonds indicates future enjoyment, probably by travel in a distant country. If you relish the almonds, every undertaking nearly will be prosperous ; if the taste is bitter, your enterprise will fail ; and the expenses of it will nearly overwhelm you.

ALTAR.—To dream you are at the altar, and receiving the holy sacrament, is a very unfavourable omen, denoting many heavy and severe afflictions. If you are in love, your lover will be taken away by death, or removed very far from you for ever. If in business, losses will be yours.

AMPUTATION.—To dream that you are having a limb cut off is a certain warning of the death of some near and dear object, wife or husband, child, parent or lover. Bereavement must certainly be your lot.

ANCHOR.—To dream of an anchor in water is a bad omen, it implies disappointment in your wishes and endeavours. To dream of an anchor part in water and part out, foretells that you will speedily have a voyage. For a young woman to dream of an anchor she will have a sailor for her husband. For a woman with child to dream of an anchor she will have a son and he will be a sailor. To dream you see an anchor difficult to weigh is a good sign denoting your abiding prosperity, and the futility of all opposition from your enemies.

ANGELS.—This is a pleasing and favourable dream. It is a sign of high enjoyment. If you dream you are with them, it indicates that you will have sweet fellowship with agreeable friends; that you will have prosperity, peace, and happiness. To a married woman it denotes she will have a numerous and virtuous family; if she dream of two angels, she will have twins the next birth. It is a happy omen to lovers; their marriage will be agreeable, and they will be surrounded with kind friends.

ANGER.—To dream you are angry with some person, it is a sign that that person is your best friend. Should you dream that your lover is angry with you be assured they love you sincerely and will make you happy.

ANGLING.—This dream betokens much affliction and trouble in your life engagements. I fear too it indicates sophistry, and design to entangle some in your meshes. Do not be guilty of such conduct. Resist the temptation that you may be delivered from evil.

ANNOY.—To dream that you are annoyed denotes that you have enemies about you.

ANTS.—Dreaming of ants it foretells your removal to a large mercantile city where you will have a numerous family of boys; that if you are industrious you may accumulate riches; but if not, you will live in poverty. To those in love it foretells a speedy marriage, and a large family. It intimates to the tradesman increase of trade and ultimate independence.

ANXIETY.—It is a dream of contrary, and denotes that your present trouble and anxiety will soon pass away.

APPAREL.—To dream that you have good rich apparel, is a dream of contrary; indicating want and penury, and great scarcity of clothes. If you dream you have no clothes is also a dream of contrary; you will have a sufficiency, if not more, of temporal things, and many changes of raiment.

APPAREL,—WHITE.—To dream you are robed in white is a sure token of your success with a lover; of success in business, or any honourable undertaking, you will find great favour with the public.

APPAREL,—BLACK.—If you go to a funeral in black, it denotes a marriage in which you and your friends are interested. But to dream of black apparel on ordinary occasions is unlucky. It denotes sickness to yourself, or family, and you will be bereaved of some one dear to you. Engage not in law-suits, for your dream portends evil, embarrassment, and difficulties; and go not any journey, for it may be unsuccessful. Are you a lover? It denotes that the object of your devotion is in trouble, unhappy, or afflicted, and likely to pay the debt of nature soon.

APPAREL,—BLUE OR PURPLE.—Denotes prosperity, happiness, and esteem, from various persons whom you wish to please. Your sweetheart is by this colour denoted very faithful, and if you marry the object of your wishes, you will experience great happiness and comfort; great success in business, approbation of friends, and much advantage by travelling.

APPAREL,—SCARLET.—By dreaming of this colour you are warned that you will experience heavy calamities, sickness, loss of friends, quarrels and disputes, originating in mere trifles; it also denotes great uneasiness by the misconduct of children.

To dream of being dressed in CRIMSON denotes that the dreamer will live to an old age, and have a moderate fortune through life; you are about to receive some pleasant news from a distant quarter; your sweetheart will leave you for some time, but afterwards will be very faithful to you.

To dream you are dressed in a variety of colours, denotes a variety of fortune will attend you. If you are in love, a quarrel will take place between you and your sweetheart, which, after some uneasiness will be settled by friends.

To dream you see another in any of the modes above described, forebodes to the party the same fortune.

To dream you are dressed in new clothes, is a favourable sign; it portends honour and success in your undertakings.

APPLES.—This is a very good dream; it indicates a long and happy life, success in business and in love. For a woman with child to dream of apples denotes that she will have a son who will be very great and wealthy.

ARROW.—To dream that an arrow is shot at you, and that it penetrates your body is a bad omen. Some person or persons are designing your ruin.

ASCEND.—To dream that you ascend a hill, and

reach the top, denotes that you will conquer your difficulties.

ASPS.—To dream of asps is a sure sign of enemies. If you dream that you tread upon them do not fear, they cannot injure you. If they run from you, you will triumph over them, but if they turn and bite you, it denotes dangerous enemies who will greatly injure you, and cause you much trouble.

ASS.—This denotes that whatever troubles or misfortunes at present afflict you, will, by patience and humility, sustain them, and that they will have a happy termination. For a young woman to dream of an ass implies that her future husband will be contented and happy, but not rich, rather headstrong, and determined to have his own way.

ASYLUM.—To dream that you are in an asylum denotes coming personal affliction. But to dream that you are merely inspecting an asylum, denotes that you will be in circumstances that will enable you to help the distressed.

BABY.—To dream that you are nursing a baby denotes sorrow and misfortune, and disappointment in love. To dream that you see a baby that is sick, foretells the death of one of the family. For a young woman to dream of having a baby, implies that she is in danger of temptation, and that she will be forsaken by her lover, and for a young man to dream that he is married, and is nursing a baby, denotes disappointment in the object of his affections, perhaps by her death.

BACHELOR.—Dreaming of a bachelor not old; portends that you will shortly meet with a lover, or friend. But to dream that you converse with an old bachelor is a sign that you are likely to die an old maid.

BACON.—To dream of eating bacon portends sorrow. To dream of buying it foretells the death of a friend, or that you will quarrel with your lover and part for ever. It predicts great trials by sickness.

BADGER.—If you dream of this animal, it is a favourable circumstance, it indicates long life and great prosperity, that you will acquire wealth by your industry, and that you will have to travel much in your own and foreign countries.

BAGPIPES.—This musical instrument seen and heard in a dream, always denotes extreme poverty, and that you will have to labour hard all your life. It also denotes that the marriage state will be unhappy, as your wife will be proud and over-bearing and not very industrious. Your marriage state will be full of cares, and very bitter.

BAKING.—To dream of baking bread, denotes sorrow, and a death in the family; or if a young person, the death or serious illness of your intended. To dream of baking pies, tarts, &c., denotes that you are to assist at a wedding, or you will be called upon to be married yourself very soon.

BALL.—If you dream that you see persons dance at a ball, and that you are engaged yourself, signifies joy, recreations, and good fellowship. It denotes the reception of a large sum of money, or very favourable intelligence. In matters of love, it foretells happiness and success, and that you will have a large family of boys and girls, which will be a comfort to you.

BALD.—To dream of baldness portends approaching sickness. For a young woman to dream that her lover is bald, foretells that he will not live to marry her. To dream that she is bald herself, implies she will be very poor, and die an old maid.

BANKRUPT.—To dream of insolvency is a dream of warning, lest you should undertake something discreditable and injurious to yourself, and opposed to the approbation of your friends. Therefore be cautious in your transactions and conduct, enter into no hasty contracts either in business or love, but seek the advice of your friends, for a step imprudently taken may embitter your future life.

BASIN.—To dream you are eating or drinking out of a basin, denotes that you will soon be in love; but without great care you will not marry the first object of your affections.

BATS.—To dream of seeing a bat flying in the air signifies that you have an enemy. If it appears flying by daylight you need not fear, but if by night, you are in danger. For a young person in love to dream of a bat denotes that you will have a dangerous rival to annoy you.

BATHING.—If you dream that you are bathing, and that the water is clear and transparent, prosperity and success in business, and in love will be yours; but if the water be dirty and muddy, you will have nothing but poverty, misfortune, sorrow, and very poor health.

BATTLE.—To dream of being in a battle implies disagreement with neighbours or friends, and with your lover of a serious nature. For a married person to dream of a battle, denotes future difficulty in obtaining temporal supplies. But if you overcome in battle, it indicates that you will baffle all the attempts of your enemies to injure you, and that success in business will be yours. In love-affairs your wishes will be realized.

BEANS.—To dream of beans is unfortunate. If you dream of eating them it foretells sickness. If you dream of seeing them growing, it foretells contention with those you love best.

BEAR.—To dream of seeing a bear, expect great vexations, and that some despotic enemy will injure you ; and that if you travel, you will meet with great hardships, but the end of your journey will be safely accomplished, and the intent accomplished. To dream that you are fighting with a bear, and kill it, is a favourable sign of your overcoming a formidable foe.

BEAUTY.—To dream that you are beautiful, is a dream of contrary, denoting that sickness will spoil your countenance, and debilitate your strength. To dream of any friend as beautiful, denotes their sickness. If you see your own and their beauty increase, it denotes death.

BED.—To dream of being in bed signifies a very early marriage to yourself ; and to dream of making a bed indicates a change of residence, and that you will live from home a long time. To dream of sitting upon a maid's bedside is certainly a sign of marriage.

BEEF.—To dream of eating beef indicates that you will always live in plenty, though you may not be rich ; but to dream of beef, and that you have not the power to eat it denotes that you will be dependent on another's bounty.

BEES.—To dream of bees is good; it denotes that your industry and enterprise in trade will be very successful. In all states of life, to dream of these insects is a good omen; to the rich, it denotes dignity and honour, and to the poor success, and a comfortable competency. To the lover it indicates happy wedlock with a virtuous, industrious, and amiable person; also it denotes a numerous family of industrious habits and amiable dispositions, proving a blessing to their parents in their declining years, and not a curse.

> To dream of bees is a rare good sign,
> For wealth and great pleasure shall be thine;
> Free shalt thou be from poverty's pain,
> All things tending to give thee gain.
>
> Look forward with joy to this blest state
> Of honour, and peace, and riches great;
> Work on, hope on, trusting in heaven,
> And all this good to thee shall be given.
>
> Thy wife shall become a fruitful vine;
> Children around thee in virtue shall shine;
> Thy life shall pass unmingled with care;
> Thy dreaming of bees denotes such fare.

BELLS.—To dream of hearing the bells ring is a fortunate sign. It is a sign of coming good news. To the young it foretells a happy and early marriage to the person so ardently loved by them. To persons in business it denotes the acquirement of a fortune. It foretells advancement in your trade or profession. If a sailor at sea dreams of hearing the bells, it augurs that his voyage will be prosperous, and that he will safely return, and marry well.

BILLIARDS.—If you dream that you are playing at billiards, it indicates that you will be placed in a difficult position, from which it will be hard to extricate yourself. If you are courting a young lady, it denotes that you will be opposed by her parents or friends.

BIRDS.—For a wealthy person to dream of birds flying, is very unlucky, it denotes a sad reverse in their circumstances. But for poor persons to dream of birds it denotes a change for the better, especially if they hear the birds singing. If the birds have a beautiful plumage, and are not frightened at you, it indicates elevation to rank and influence.

BIRD'S NEST.—To dream of finding a bird's nest containing eggs, is a sign that you will have property left. If there are young ones in, you will have a lawsuit about it and lose it.

BIRTH.—For a married woman to dream of giving birth to a child portends that she will get well over her confinement. For a single young woman to dream the same denotes that she is in danger of losing her chastity.

BLACKBERRIES.—To dream that you are gathering blackberries to eat, indicates approaching sickness. If you see others gathering them, you have enemies where you least expect them, and who will strive to injure you in your business.

BLEEDING.—To dream of bleeding in any part of your person is a very unhappy dream ; especially if you dream it cannot be stopped ; it is the sign of protracted illness, and debility through life.

BLIND.—For persons in love to dream that they are blind, denotes that they have made a bad choice in the object of their affections ; and that their connection will by some unexpected cause come to an end. To dream of the blind is a sign that you will have few real friends.

BLOOD.—To dream of blood is very bad, if you see it upon yourself; if on others, it denotes a sudden death to some of the family, loss of property, and severe disappointment. If expecting to be married, something will occur to prevent your union, and if you dream that your hands are bloody, you will be in danger of injuring some person. Beware!

BOAT.—If you dream that you are sailing in a boat or ship and the water is smooth and the weather pleasant, it is a lucky omen, denoting a prosperous business, and happiness in the marriage state. If the water is rough and muddy you will have to labour all your life. If you fall into the water you will meet hereafter with great peril.

BONES.—Dreaming of bones denotes poverty; if they are partly clothed with flesh, that you will grow rich by degrees, and ultimately possess a good deal of property. To dream of human bones foretells that you will become rich through the death of some relative or friend.

BOOKS.—To dream of books is a good sign; it denotes that your future life will be very agreeable. If a woman in the family way dreams that she sees a number of books, it betokens the birth of a son who will rise to eminent learning and great honour. For young woman to dream of books indicates that she will be married to a very learned man.

BOOTS.—If you dream that you are wearing a new pair of boots and they hurt your feet, it is a sign that you will meet with great and painful difficulties caused by your own imprudence.

BOTTLE.—To dream of a bottle full of wine indicates your future prosperity; if the bottle be empty, it denotes that you have an enemy in possession of a secret, which if revealed, will do you a deal of harm. To dream that you are drinking out of a bottle denotes that you are intending mischief on some young person, and which, if perpetrated will greatly injure your character.

BOWER.—To dream you are seated in a bower portends that you will overcome every obstacle to your happiness. If in a bower with your lover, indicates that your lover is sincere and faithful; speedy marriage, and great happiness in that state.

BOW AND ARROW.—To dream that you are shooting with a bow and arrow, and that you hit the target, denotes that your future well-organized plans will succeed above all you could have imagined; if you miss the target, that your schemes are not well organized, and that the object of your ambition will be blasted. If a young woman dreams that her lover is shooting with a bow and arrow, it foretells her that he is a restless fickle being, always changing his plans and pursuits, to gain money which he will never acquire.

BOX.—If you dream that you are opening a box, and looking for something in it, and cannot find it, it is an indication that you are going to be troubled about money matters; or that you will suffer some pecuniary lost.

BOX.—To dream of the plant "Box," implies long life and prosperity, with a happy marriage and large family, to be your solace in old age.

BRACELET.—To dream that you are wearing a

bracelet, you will shortly be married to a wealthy person. If you dream that you find a bracelet it is a sign of a coming fortune; if you dream that some one put upon your hand a bracelet you will soon fall in love, and be accepted, or if already in love, you will be married without delay.

BRAMBLES.—To dream of briars and brambles and that you are injured by them, is a very unlucky dream, it denotes many difficulties, and poverty and privation all your life. If you are not hurt by them, you will have trouble but of a short duration.

BRANCH.—If you dream that you see a tree full of branches, it denotes abundance, and a numerous family,—a happy posterity.

BREAD.—To dream of seeing a quantity of bread is a sign of competency in temporal things. If you dream of eating good bread, you will enjoy good health, and live long; but if the bread is burned or sad, it is a bad sign, and generally portends a funeral. To dream of baking bread is also bad, generally denoting affliction, and sorrow.

TO BREAK.—To dream of any breakage is unlucky. If you dream of breaking any of your limbs it is a sign of approaching sickness. If you dream of breaking tables or chairs, or any article of furniture, it indicates insolvency. If you dream of breaking a window, it forebodes a robbery, or danger from fire. If you dream of breaking a looking glass, it implies the death of a relative, neighbour, or friend. To dream of breaking earthenware or glass, denotes a robbery by a servant; and if a woman dreams of breaking her wedding-ring it portends the death of her husband.

BREAST.—To dream that you are reclining on the breast of another, is a sign of true, valuable, lasting friendship, and affection.

BREATH.—To dream you are out of breath, or have difficult breathing is a sign that your health is about to give way.

BREWING.—If you dream that you are brewing, you may expect the visit of some distant friend. It denotes also great efforts to secure your honourable purposes, and that you shall succeed, and for a short time have both trouble and uneasiness, but all will end happily.

BRIDE, BRIDESMAID, OR BRIDEGROOM.—This is a dream of contrary. To dream that you take any of these characters is very unlucky, it is a sure forerunner of grief and disappointment, and that the dreamer will soon have to be chief mourner at a funeral of some dear friend, or acquaintauce.

BRIDGE.—To dream that you are crossing a bridge in the day time, foretells a change of situation. If any person interrupts you, it implies that your lover will deceive you; but if you pass along without any impediment, you will succeed in your undertakings, and prosper. If you dream that you are walking towards a bridge that is broken down, be not hasty to make any change in your situation for the present, as you will not be successful.

BUGLE.—To dream that you are playing this instrument, is a token of joy, occasioned by great friendship and kindness from your relatives. To dream of hearing a bugle sound denotes unexpected news from abroad of a very pleasing nature; and to married persons it denotes the birth of a child.

BUGS.—To dream of these filthy vermin, is a sure indication of sickness, and of many enemies seeking to injure you. To a young man it implies that his enemies are trying to deprive him of his situation. To a young woman, that she has several rivals who do not hesitate to traduce her character. To a merchant or tradesman, it denotes that he has servants or persons in his employment who are robbing him, and injuring him to a great extent.

BUILDINGS.—If you dream of seeing a large number of new buildings, it indicates that you will shortly remove to a distant place, where you will be far happier, and escape the design of some secret enemies. If the buildings are large and magnificent, you will be prosperous and happy ; If they are palaces, it prognosticates much wealth and honour. But if they appear small, mean, and dilapidated, your circumstances will be indigent. If the buildings are only partly built, and you inquire why they are not finished, and no one can tell you, it is a sign that your plans are difficult to accomplish, and that you will die while they are incomplete.

BULL.—To dream that you are pursued by a mad bull, denotes that you have violent enemies, and that many injurious reports will be spread detrimental to your character ; and that you will be in danger of losing your friends. If in love, your intended will be in some great danger, and will narrowly escape some dreadful misfortune.

BURNS.—A dream of contrary, implying health, happiness and warm friendship.

BUTTER.—To dream of butter, in any way, or form, is a good dream and indicates joy and feasting. To the lover it is a sign of early marriage. In litigation it betokens success; also in any controversy, or dispute. Your absent friend, if you have one, will come home safely, and be to you a friend in need. If you are exposed to any trial or danger, it betokens speedy deliverance.

BUTTER-MILK.—To dream of drinking butter-milk implies that your intended has but an irritable and unamiable temper, or that you will be disappointed in love; that your rival will take your lover from you. To a married person it denotes losses, sorrow and mourning. To a farmer, an uncongenial season, and loss of crops, if he dreams of seeing butter-milk in large quantities it indicates losses, but that he will overcome them.

CABBAGE.—To dream of cutting cabbages denotes that your wife, or lover, or husband, as the case may be, is very jealous of you. If you dream of some one else cutting them, it is a sign that you have an enemy trying to create jealousy in the mind of your beloved. If you dream of eating cabbage, it denotes the sickness of the object of your affections, and that you will have severe losses and loss of a sum of money.

CAB.—To dream of riding in a cab denotes a short sickness, and speedy recovery by change of climate. It also denotes increasing prosperity.

CAGE.—To dream that you see birds in a cage is a sign that you will have an early and an agreeable marriage. If you dream you see a cage, the door open, and no bird there, it is a sign that your lover will forsake you; and it is much if ever you be married. To dream of seeing a person letting a bird escape from its cage, is a sign of an elopement.

CAKES.—If you dream of oat-cakes, it denotes health and strength; if of sweet cakes, of coming joy; if of making spicy cakes and bread, an approaching marriage, at which you will be, and meet with your lover who will receive you with open arms. To dream of cakes twice, denotes your own marriage in which you will be happy both day and night.

CALM.—To dream of a calm succeeding a storm indicates the reconciliation of separated friends; the end of trouble; the commencement of peace.

CALUMNY.—To dream that you are calumniated, is a dream of contrary, denoting that you will be generally and highly respected.

CAMELS.—To dream of these wonderfully hard and patient creatures, denotes that heavy burdens will press upon you, that you will be hardly dealt with, meet with many disasters, all which you will bear with heroism; but the time will come when you will be entirely emancipated, and become very happy.

CANARY BIRD.—If you dream that you hear a Canary sing, it denotes your marriage, and a comfortable habitation. It denotes that your partner will be cheerful and tender and very kind to you. If a married woman dreams she sees two canaries in a cage, it prognosticates twins.

CANDLES.—To dream that you are making candles, denotes that you will be very useful to others; if you dream that you are buying candles, it indicates feasting and rejoicing. To dream that you see a candle burning brightly, portends that you will receive a letter containing pleasing intelligence: but if you dream that you see a candle snuffed or blown out, it denotes the death of a friend or near relative,

CANNON.—To dream of hearing the firing of cannon, denotes national war, and personal trouble and vexation. To a young woman it denotes her future husband will have been a soldier.

CAPTIVE.—To dream of becoming a captive is a sign of insolvency, and imprisonment for debt. It is also a sign of an unhappy marriage, suffering from the bad disposition and misconduct of the wife or husband, as the case may be.

CAP.—To dream of a female with a fine cap is a sign that she is in love with you. But she would make a foolish wife. To dream you see a man with a cap on, denotes that your lover is a silly fellow, and will care but little for you after the honeymoon.

CART.—To dream of riding in a cart denotes that you will come down in the world, and have many hard changes. To dream of driving a cart indicates poverty and great straits.

CARVING.—To dream that you are carving meat for others denotes that you will be a benefactor; and to be carving meat for yourself denotes prosperity in your trade; if single, that you will succeed in love.

CARPET.—To dream that you are in a carpeted room denotes advancement to a state of riches.

CARRIAGE.—If you dream of riding in a carriage, it is a dream of contrary, and betokens a state of poverty.

CATS.—An unfavourable dream, denoting treachery and deceit. If a young woman dreams of cats it is a sign that her lover is sly and very deceitful; if a

young man dreams of cats, she whom he loves will
be a vixen, and will be sure to wear the breeches.
If a tradesman dreams of cats, it denotes bad and
dishonest servants. To dream of a cat and kittens
is a sign of a numerous family, but not too good ;
trifling and vain. To dream that you kill a cat is
an omen that you will discover your enemies, and
defeat their purposes.

CATTLE.—If you dream of cattle grazing in a
pasture, it is a good sign of prosperty and affluence.
If you dream of driving cattle it portends that if
you are diligent and industrious, you will amass a
great fortune. Black and large horned cattle denote
numerous and violent enemies.

CATHEDRAL.—To dream that you are in a cathedral denotes that you will have a competency, to
enable you to travel and see antiquities. To married
persons, it denotes good children, some of whom will
be eminent in the church.

CHAINS.—To dream you see chains is a token that
enemies are concerting to harm you, but that you
will escape their meshes. If you dream that you
are confined in chains, it betokens very severe trials
for a time, from which you will in time be extricated.
To dream that a person puts a gold chain upon your
neck indicates great favour ; and to the lover conjugal union and felicity.

CHAMBERMAID.—To a man, this intimates marriage with a high and arbitrary dame, and that he
will have to knuckle under.

CHAFF.—This dream indicates that your schemes
are not well-formed, and they will prove abortive ;
and if you love, the person whom you love will

prove empty-headed, notwithstanding great pretensions and *bumpkum*.

CHEESE.—To dream of Cheese denotes deception and infidelity in a lover. If the cheese be mity, it denotes numerous little meddling persons who will annoy you. To dream of eating cheese betokens regret for having acted imprudently.

CHERRIES.—To dream of cherries in winter implies disappointment in business, and in the marriage state, and deceit in love.

CHILDREN.—If a married woman dreams of her confinement, it denotes that she will soon be convalescent, and have a healthy child. If a single woman dreams of having a child, her virtue will be threatened.

CHICKENS.—To dream of a hen and chickens is the forerunner of ill luck; your lover will desert you, and marry another. To a farmer, it denotes a bad season.

CHILDREN.—This is a lucky dream, and denotes success in trade, and increase of wealth; to dream that you see your child die, is a dream of contrary; the child will recover.

CHURCH.—To dream that you go to church in mourning, denotes a wedding; if you go in white, it denotes a funeral.

CHURNING.—To dream that you are churning, is a sign of prosperity and plenty. To the single, it portends a happy marriage. To the farmer, a good season and good crops, and to all it is an omen of abundance and good health.

CLOCK.—To dream you hear the clock strike denotes a speedy marriage, and that you will be very comfortable in life. To dream that you are counting the hours, if in the forenoon, it indicates much happiness; but if in the afternoon, that misfortune and danger will attend you; that your false lover doats upon another. If the clock strikes roughly, and not the full hours, it denotes the failure of your health, and probably your death.

CLOUDS.—To dream of dark clouds suspended over you, it indicates that you will have to pass through great sorrows sufficient to overwhelm you. But if the clouds break, and roll away, your sorrows will pass away, and prosperity be your lot.

CLOTHES.—If you dream that you have plenty of clothes is a dream of contrary; you will want clothing. If you dream that you are naked, it is a sign that you will be well clothed. For a woman to dream that she is making children's clothes, is a sign of a particular state. If a sailor dreams that he has lost his clothes by shipwreck, it is a sign of marriage.

CLOVER.—" I do not know a better dream than this," says old Ptolemy. If you are in a field of clover, it is an omen that you will do well, be in health, and very happy. Art thou in love? Well shalt thou succeed. Thy wife shall be thy comfort always, and thy family shall prosper. To dream this, thou art highly favoured. If you are in love nothing can be more favourable, and all your undertakings will prosper and be advantageous to you. To the lover it also foretells that his intended wife will have great wealth and many children.

COFFEE.—This dream is favourable. It denotes settlement in life, prosperity, great happiness in the married state. To a single person it promises a faithful, affectionate, and confiding lover.

COFFIN.—It is a bad dream. It is a sign of the death of some dear friend; that death will rob the lover of the one so dear to him. As to the community, it is a sign of great mortality.

COLD.—This is a dream of contrary. It denotes comfort in your circumstances; kind and loving friends; you may have short trials, but you will happily surmount them.

COLLIERY AND COALS.—To dream that you are near a coalpit, denotes that you will be exposed to danger, and to dream that you are in a coalpit, is a sign that you cannot escape. Affliction is sure to follow dreaming of coals; losses in trade, and disappointment in love. To see coals burning bright and clear is favourable, the love of your intended is sincere. If you dream that the coals are extinguished, it foretells your own death, or that of a friend.

COLOURS.—Dreaming of colours, flags, and banners streaming in the air denotes elevation from obscurity, and that you will be highly honoured and esteemed.

COMBAT.—To dream of a combat with any one, denotes rivalry, and that you will seek revenge. If you dream that your combat ends in victory, it is a sign that you will retain the affections of your lover.

COMETS.—" I never dreamed of a comet," says old Ptolemy, " but it portended great calamity among the nations, as war, famine, and plague, and even cold-blooded murder. All persons, after such a dream may look for misfortune. It signifies descent from every situation to a lower. If you dream of a comet, do not travel, nor expose yourself where danger is, nor undertake any hazardous enterprise. If you do you will suffer."

COMMUNION.—To dream that you are partaking of bread and wine in church or chapel, is at all times favourable, it foretells many enjoyments. To the maiden it denotes virtuous love in him with whom she associates.

COMPANION.—To dream of your companion denotes abiding friendship.

CONCUBINE.—If you dream of speaking to a concubine, indicates that you sink into immorality, lose your character, and awfully suffer in consequence. It is a bad dream to you, very.

CONCERT.—To dream of a concert is a dream of contrary, denoting wrangling and disputation—disagreement among relations.

COOKING.—Dreaming of cooking denotes a convivial party, and also a wedding of some friend. It also denotes a family made happy by the abundance of this world's good.

CORKS.—To dream that you are corking bottles, indicates that soon you will have cause to make an entertainment on account of a favourable change in your circumstances. If you draw corks, it is a sign of the visit of some particular friend.

CORN-FIELD.—"To dream of cornfields, or corn," says Ptolemy, "is a most favourable omen. It betokens health, a happy family, a prosperous trade, great wealth. Thy speculations shall prosper. Art thou a tiller of the soil? Well shalt thou succeed. Dost thou ply the great deep in thy ships? Favourable breezes shall be thine, and large well-paying

freights. Art thou a lover? Thy life shall be a
perennial honey-moon. Well hast thou dreamed.
Thine old age shall be green and happy. I congrat-
ulate thee on thy dream, whoever thou art!"

CORPSE.—To dream you see a corpse predicts a
hasty, inconsiderate, and imprudent marriage, in which
the parties will be very unhappy; they will be unequally yoked together. The children will be
unhealthy, have bad dispositions, to make it a family
of misery.

COW.—To dream that you are pursued by a cow,
denotes an enemy; if you escape it, you will defeat
your enemy. To dream of milking a cow is a sign
of abundance. If a woman dreams of a cow calving,
its a sign of a difficult confinement.

CRABS.—To dream of a crab denotes reverses, and
to a sailor danger of shipwreck, and drowning.

CROWN.—To dream of a monarch's crown, denotes
favour with the great, and elevation in your state.
To dream that you wear a royal crown is a dream
of contrary; it denotes your degradation. To dream
that you give a crown, shows that you will rise to
independance.

CROWS.—This is a sign of a funeral.

CRUCIFIX.—To dream of holding a crucifix indicates trials and crosses. If you hold it long, it denotes heroism in your future misfortunes.

CUCKOO.—This dream denotes temporary disappointments in love, even a rupture; but eventually
you will secure by marriage the person whom you
love. If you dream that you hear the cuckoo, and
she stutters, it denotes that you will not succeed in

business or love. To the married it is the omen of widowhood.

CUCUMBERS.—This is a dream of contrary. As cucumbers are deemed unwholesome, it denotes health; for the afflicted to dream of cucumbers, it denotes speedy restoration to health. To a single person, it denotes a happy engagement, and eventually an agreeable marriage.

DAIRY. — To dream that you are in a dairy, making butter, denotes that you will be very fortunate in your secular concerns; that you will marry a plain homely person, and be happy and have many children.

DARK.—If you dream that you are in darkness and cannot find your way, and you stumble, it denotes a change in your temporal affairs for the worse; by your imprudence, you will dreadfully commit yourself. But if you dream that you emerge from the darkness, and behold the sun, it denotes your ultimate escape; you will be happy, and regain your reputation.

DANCE.—This is a favourable dream; it indicates that you will be the recipient of great favour and honour; that your plans will succeed; that in love you will win the hand of a valuable person.

DEAD.—To dream of your relatives and friends who are dead, denotes personal or relative affliction, and also much mental suffering. If you dream that they are happy, it is a sign favourable to you.

DEATH.—This is a dream of contrary; it augurs happy long life. To the single it denotes an honourable and happy marriage. If a sick person dreams of death, it portends death.

DEER.—This is an unfavourable dream. It portends quarrels and dissensions in which you will be a party. If in trade it denotes embarrassment and failure, ending in imprisonment. It is a bad dream for the tradesman, the merchant, the sailor, and all official characters.

DESERT.—To dream that you are travelling across a desert, is a sign of a difficult and dangerous journey, especially if you dream that the weather is wet and boisterous. If you see the sun shine, your journey, and all affairs will be safe and prosperous.

DEVIL.—This is a shocking dream; and I fear that those who dream of him, are too much akin to him. It is high time for them to mend; for this dream portends great evil which the "father of lies" will bring upon them. It is better to pursue virtue, which is devil's bane.

DEVOTION.—To dream that you are devotional, and at your devotions is a good sign of bodily health, and temporal happiness.

DIAMOND.—This dream indicates solid and extensive wealth. Ptolemy says, "Dreaming of a diamond thou lover, thy wife will be a diamond to thee, very precious; right happy shalt thou be. Man of commerce, if thou dreamest of diamonds great quantities of gold will roll into thy lap. Seamen and sailors, dream away about diamonds, for it betokens to you great good. Barren woman, dream of diamonds, and children thou shalt have, and good ones too."

DICE.—To dream that you are playing with dice, is a sign of great changes in your business and circumstances; it betokens your life to be much chequered; and your enterprises very hazardous.

Let the female look well to the private character of her lover. Is he a gambler? There lies her danger. To a young man, it denotes that he will lose the respect of those upon whom he is dependant.

DINNER.—If you dream that you are getting your dinner, it is a dream of contrary. It foretells straits and difficulties, and that you will often want a meal. You will not be comfortable in the married life. Your wife and children will be a source of pain to you.

DIRT.—To dream that your person or clothes are dirty, denotes sickness and sorrow. It also implies loss of virtue and reputation. To dream that one throws dirt upon you, is a sign that enemies will try to injure your character. Beware of some in whom you are so confiding.

DISASTER.—It is a dream of contrary; you will hear of the exaltation of some friend in whom you are interested, and it will lead to a marriage. What! if it be you? To dream of disasters at sea portends a prosperous voyage. It is a favourable dream for a man of business.

DISEASE.—To dream that you are diseased, it is a sign to a sick person of recovery; to the young man it is a warning against evil company, and intemperance. It is not a favourable dream for lovers. It denotes infidelity. If any have a law-suit, this dream is a bad omen.

DISPUTE.—Disputes always foretell quarrels and dissensions, and impediments to your success in trade; yet all will be of short continuance, you will surmount every trial. To a lover, to dream of disputes betoken some disagreement, which it will be difficult to make up.

DISTANCE.—To dream that you are at a distance from your friends, foretells family quarrels, and alienation. To dream of any friend at a distance, indicates that you will agreeably hear of them shortly.

DITCH.—To dream of ditches is unfavourable. It betokens great danger, great losses, great injuries, and many malignant enemies coming upon you. The lover who dreams that he or she falls into a ditch, is a sign that the contemplated marriage will be a bad one. For a tradesman to dream of falling into a ditch, it is a sign of bankruptcy.

DIVING-BELL.—To dream of a diving-bell is a happy omen; it indicates every kind of happiness—a brisk trade—a joyful family; and if in love, a successful consummation by marriage. You will be rich, virtuous, and honoured.

DIVORCE.—This is a dream of contrary. If a married person dreams of sueing for a divorce, it is a sign of the fidelity of his or her partner, and that he has no cause for jealousy.

DOLPHINS.—This is not a good dream. It indicates the death of some friend at sea; and the shipwreck of a vessel in which you are interested; the failure of the bright hopes of a lover; that your present prospects are futile; they will all be blasted; if you travel, it denotes great danger.

DOCKS.—To dream that you are standing by the docks in a sea-port town, denotes you will hear favourable news from abroad.

DOGS.—If you dream that a dog fondles with you, you will meet with faithful friends. But if he bites you, your best friend from some cause, will become your greatest enemy. If it only barks at you, you will quarrel with your friend or lover, and they will seek to injure you but in vain.

DOVES.—This is a fortunate dream. It denotes progressive prosperity in business; permanent esteem and affection of friends, peace in the family. If you love, your love will be warmly returned. If you hear the voice of a turtle-dove, it is an omen of the death of a dear friend. If you see in your dream a dove shot, and fall to the ground, it is a sign of your own death. To the lover it denotes that his love is returned with all the fervour he could desire, that he will marry and be very happy for many years, but that he will lose his wife and die a widower. It indicates the same to a young woman, with the exception that she will be left a widow at an early age.

DOWER.—If you dream of receiving a dower, it is a sign that the riches of your intended is nothing but a pretence to possess you. It is a dream of contrary.

DRAUGHTS.—To dream of playing at draughts is a sign that you have no fixity about you; that you are whimsical and given to change, and will never prosper till your loose course is altered. To dream of playing at draughts is not a good sign for any; it denotes poverty, unhappiness, and uncertainty, alternation of wealth and misery; that love too will alternate, first warm, hot, then cold.

DRESS.—To dream of buying a dress, denotes advancement; and that you will obtain your wishes. To dream of being well dressed is a sign of the approval of your friends and lover.

DRINK.—To dream that you are drinking at a fountain, is a sign of much happiness and enjoyment. If the water is muddy, it denotes approaching trouble. If you are thirsty, and cannot find water, it portends that your trials will have to be borne without any assistance. You will need self-reliance. To dream that you give drink to the thirsty foretells your sympathetic heart and your benefactions when required.

DRIVING.—If you dream of driving a gig, expect losses in trade. To dream that some one is driving you in a carriage is a good sign ; it foretells a marriage. If you dream of driving any vehicle, it betokens your dependance, and poverty. To dream of driving an ass, is a sign that you will be tyrannical with your husband or wife, as the case may be.

DROPSY.—To dream of dropsy, denotes great bodily sickness, and aberration of mind, nearly insanity ; it portends suicide by drowning, or casual drowning at sea. Let the dreamer be very careful and watchful.

DROWN.—To dream that you are drowning denotes overwhelming difficulties, losses in trade, and by death. If you dream you are drowning, and some one, or a life-boat, &c. rescues you, it is a sign that some friend will efficiently help you in your difficulties and sorrows.

DRUM.—To dream you hear the sound of a drum, with its musical accompaniments is a sign of national and family turmoils, and disorders, and that the country will be afflicted with war.

DRUNK.—To dream that you are drunk, denotes your fall into prodigality and ruin, and that you will be reckless of your substance, reputation, and domestic comfort. If a female dreams she sees a drunken man, it is a sign that her future husband will be intemperate.

DUCKS.—"I know that this dream is fortunate and unfortunate," says an ancient astrologer; "if you see the ducks flying, it is an omen of the increase of riches; if you see them swimming, on the glassy water; it is a good sign to the merchant, to the artizan, and to his family; and he or she who loves may calculate on falling into the lap of peace, and plenty. If you see them dive and bring up worms, it denotes a life of drudgery and servile dependance. To dream that you see a duck and a drake augurs that your wished for marriage will soon take place.

DUMB.—Dreaming of being dumb, portends that you will so demean yourself as to be devoid of all apology.

DUST.—To dream that you are almost blinded with dust, indicates the failure of your business, and the dispersion of your family. But if in your dream you get clear of it, you will recover your former state.

DWARF.—This is a dream of contrary. If you dream you see a dwarf, it is a sign that you will be elevated in rank. If you dream that you are a dwarf, it denotes health, muscular strength, and independent and commanding circumstances. To the tradesman, the farmer, and the lover, it is a lucky dream.

EARTHQUAKE.—This foretells much trouble to the dreamer: it indicates great losses in trade, bereavement; family ties death will dissolve; it also denotes family quarrels, the interruption of domestic happiness.

I fear too it is a sign of national calamities, commercial distress, and probably war. It augurs the dissolution of the lover's bond, and heart-breaking agony.

EARWIG.—An enemy! He will threaten to undermine the basis of your prosperity and happiness. He works very secretly.—A rival! a rival! Mind he does not covertly steal the heart of your lover.

EATING.—To dream that you are eating is an unfortunate omen, portending family quarrels, separations of lovers, losses in trade, bad harvest, and shipwrecks at sea. To dream that you sea other persons eating and you with them, denotes choice friendship, and eminent success in your trade or profession. In the conjugal state, you will be very happy, loving your wife, and be loved by her.

ECHO.—To dream you hear an echo to your own voice denotes that the letter you have sent will be met by a favourable answer, that the person to whom you have proposed will accept you; that your children will be beautiful and lovely, and good. Mind you do not idolize these little echoes! You will also hear of an absent friend.

ECLIPSE.—Old Ptolemy says this is a strange dream. "Man of ambition," says he, "hoping thy rich relation would leave thee a fortune; thy hope is eclipsed; for another has supplanted thee. Man of ease, expect to hear, according to thy dream of the death of thy parents, or other fraternity. Thou doatest on thy wife, or husband, or child, as the case may be; but death is coming; thy sun of happiness shall be eclipsed. Loving swain, gentle maiden, I know what ye like best,—marriage; it shall not be; ye dreamed of an eclipse; your hopes are darkened. Hope is fled. O confiding one, thy friend is a traitor and all thy expectations from him are obscured. A change, a change in every department of thy life—a reverse is prognosticated by thy dream of an eclipse! Learn wisdom therefore."

EDUCATION.—To dream of education in any way denotes your advance in literary fame. You will be much esteemed.

EGGS.—To dream of seeing a great number of eggs, indicates success in trade and in love. It also denotes a happy marriage and good children, and great prosperity. Do you hope for advancement to a better station, or office, it shall be yours. To dream that the eggs prove rotten denotes unfaithful and treacherous friends and lovers. To dream of eating eggs portends great enjoyment.

ELDERBERRIES.—To dream of this fruit portends sickness and death. It denotes a very uncertain courtship.

ELEPHANT.—To dream of an elephant denotes health, and strength; and that you will associate with the respectable of society.

ELOPEMENT.—To dream that you are eloping with your lover, indicates an unhappy marriage state; prognosticating much discomfort, if not misery. You will have a bad partner. That your spouse will be thoughtless and extravagant in all things, as well as hasty and quarrelsome in disposition. If you dream that your lover has eloped with some one else, the sooner you break that engagement the better; for your rival is likely to supplant you. To dream of a relative or friend eloping denotes their marriage, and unless you quickly come to some definite understanding, you will be supplanted. To dream of some friend or acquaintance eloping, is a sign of a sudden death.

EMBROIDERY.—To dream of embroidery, denotes deceit in those who apparently love you.

EMPLOY.—To dream that you want employment is a sign of prosperity. To dream that you have abundance of employment, denotes that you will have nothing to do. To dream that you employ others, is a sign that, if you are not mindful, you will injure them. This is a dream of contrary.

ENTERTAINMENT.—To dream of a place of entertainment, is the forerunner of some joyful festivity, where you will come in contact with your intended, and heart will meet heart. If you felt great pleasure in your dream, marriage will soon crown your wishes. If you felt unwilling to leave the entertainment, your marriage will be a very happy one. It is a good dream for the merchant, and tradesman. To the sailor it betokens a prosperous voyage, and a safe return, and to the soldier safety in battle.

ENVY.—To dream that you are envied is a sign that you will be admired and loved; and that if you have a rival, he will yet be utterly confounded. This is a dream of contrary.

EPICURE.—To dream that you see an epicure, portends that you will see a sick friend; if you dream that you are an epicure, it denotes your own sickness.

ERMINE.—To dream you see any one arrayed in this beautiful and expensive fur, portends that you will rise to great honour and dignity. If you dream that you are arrayed in ermine, it denotes a great and magnificent state awaiting you.

ESCAPE.—To dream that you try to escape from any danger, and cannot denotes continued trouble. To dream that you escape from sickness, from an enemy, from fire and water is a good sign; you must have trouble for a season; but eventually you will be delivered. If you escape from a serpent, depend upon it, it behoves you to enquire into the character of your lover. Is the party a snake in the grass? If so, escape for thy life.

EVERGREENS.—Lasting happiness! lasting love! lasting honour! perennial domestic bliss. Fresh engagements will be crowned with success. Speak to her! Speak to him, and the golden knot is tied. Enter the ship, cross the sea; safely shalt thou return. Go to new position, change thy residence; thou shalt be happy. Thy dream is of an Evergreen.

EXILE.—If you dream that you are banished, it implies that you will have to travel much.

FABLES.—If you dream that you are reading, telling, or hearing fables, it denotes that you will have agreeable friends, with whom you will have very agreeable association. To a lover it indicates that his or her intended is dissatisfied with you.

FACES.—If you dream that you see your own face in a glass, it is a sign that your secret plans will be discovered, and that you will fall into condemnation. If you see in dreaming many strange faces, it portends a change of your present abode, and associations. If you gaze in your dream upon the faces of friends, &c., it is a sign of a party, or wedding, to which you will be invited.

FAILURE.—To deam that you fail in business—

that you fail in securing the person that you love—
that your plans answer not,—is a dream of contrary;
it indicates that, by wise and cautious procedure, in
all things you will succeed.

FAIR.—It is very unlucky to dream of being at a
fair, it portends negligence in your business, and its
failure, and also false friends. The persons about
you are not so honest as they should be. Through
rivalry the lover is likely to suffer loss.

FAIRY.—"To dream that you see a fairy," says
Sergeius, the ancient astrologer, "is a very favourable
dream. Beggars have had this dream, and afterwards
become very rich. Swains and maidens have come
to me, and related this dream, and I have said,
Happy man! a noble wife for thee, and a rich
dowry too: happy woman! thou wilt find a husband
indeed. The first month of thy delicious enjoyment,
shall go through every month of every year, and
many years, of thy happy life! The labouring man,
the trader, who dreams this dream shall rapidly rise
into independence. And the bearing woman shall be
safely delivered."

FALCON.—This is a very bad dream. There is a
foe near you, full of envy, very near you, injuring
you with the tongue, and mind he or she does not
injure you with the hands. Art thou loving a person?
There is one intending to rob thee.

FALL.—To dream that you fall from an eminence,
from a tree, or the edge of a precipice, denotes a
loss of situation, and of property. If you are in love,
you bestow your attachments in vain; you will never
marry the person. To the tradesman, it denotes a
failing business, embarrassment, &c. To the sailor it
denotes a stormy voyage and shipwreck

FALSE.—" I never heard of any one dreaming that he met with false friends," says old Ptolemy, "but it indicated the very reverse; true, firm, and lasting friendship; a lover not of mushroom growth, but like an evergreen, always perennial!"

FAMINE.—This is a dream of contrary, denoting national prosperity, and individual comfort, in wealth and much enjoyment. You will have many friends, a true lover, and a happy family.

FARM.—To dream that you are taking a farm, denotes advancement. Probably some will bequeath property to you, and make you independent. If you dream of visiting a farm, and of partaking of its produce, it is a sign of good health. If you are single and unengaged, and a young person there serves you with something to eat and drink, you will soon be in love very agreeably. If a very old person is only seen, you may see in that old bachelorism or old maidism.

FARTHING.—To dream that you are not worth a farthing, or that some one gives you a farthing is a positive dream of evil. It portends a coming down in the world.

FAT.—" I once dreamed that I was getting fat," says old Quinsey, the astrologer, "and it was followed by a bad illness; and my wife Lucretia had the same dream, and she fell into a violent fever. My son, Ibeera, had a similar dream, and he had a fracas with his lover; they separated, and the false one wed another. Yea, this is a dream inspired by Sathanas, an intimation that the evil spirit meditates you ill."

FATHER.—To dream of your father, denotes that he loves you; if he be dead, it is a sign of affliction.

FAWN.—For a young man or young woman to dream of a young deer, is a sign of inconstancy. If a married woman has such a dream, it portends fruitfulness.

FEASTING.—This is an unfavourable dream, portending disappointments, enemies, and great lowness of spirit. Mind you are not thrown down on a bed of sickness. Ardent lover, dreaming of wedding thy dear one, this dreaming of feasting is bad for thee. A rival, even death ; will frustrate thy intentions.

FIDDLE.—This dream is a sign of prosperity, and of great enjoyment. You will receive joyful intelligence of a beloved distant friend. It is a sign that your lover will be accepted, and his suite will issue in happy wedlock—an agreeable companion, and good children. To the sailor it betokens a prosperous voyage, and return to the arms of his faithful lover. To dream that you are tuning and playing the fiddle, denotes your speedy marriage. If in your dream the strings break, you will never wed.

FIELDS.—To dream that you are walking in green fields, augurs very great prosperity, and agreeable circumstances, whether in trade or in love. To dream of being in withered or scorched fields, denotes coming poverty. To dream that you are in clover fields, or barley and wheat fields, and the crops are luxuriant, it denotes very great wealth, and agreeable connexions. If you dream that you are in a field newly ploughed and harrowed, denotes that success is before you ; but that you will have to make many sacrifices, and to be very indefatigable previously. If you are about a situation, be sure you will get it and be very comfortable. If you dream of being in a meadow or clover field, you will marry a rich and very handsome person, and will have many lovely children who will grow up very accomplished. Such a dream is a sure prognosticator of happiness in love and marriage, and great success in business and speculation. On the other hand, to dream of being in a ploughed field denotes great trouble, sorrow, and deprivation, and a very hard struggle through life for a decent livelihood.

FIGS.—This is a favourable dream, denoting that you are likely to receive a munificent gift which will raise you to comparative independance.

FIGHTING.—This dream certainly portends disagreements and quarrels in families. It also denotes misunderstandings among lovers, if not temporary separation. If you dream that a person fights you and beats you, it is a sign that the malice of your enemies will be successful; if you beat him, that you will defeat the malignant policy of your foes. It is a bad dream for the merchant, the soldier, and the sailor.

FILBERTS.—To dream of eating good ripe filberts indicates that a sick person will recover; and to a person in health it denotes the continuance of the same, and that he will live to an old age. It is a very favourable omen for the lover, portending the speedy nuptial ceremony. If you dream that the shell is empty, or that the kernel is worm-eaten, it is a bad omen—of false and disappointed hopes, and pretending friends. The lover will have to mourn over the falsehearted.

FIRE.—"Thou hast dreamed of fire, hast thou?" said Benevant, the great astrologer; "why, thou hast had a luck dream. It betokens for thee health and great happiness, kind relations, and warm friends. And if a young dame or hind, or lady and gentle-

man should thus dream, then that which you sigh
for, crave, and weep for, marriage, shall soon be
yours. Be patient a little! But if you dream that
you are burned with the fire; it portends calamity.

FISHING.—To dream that you are fishing and
obtain no fish, is an omen of bad success in business,
or in love. If you angle them, it augurs the acquisition of riches. If you see the fishes at the bottom
of the water, it being very clear, it is a sign of
wealth and grandeur.

FISH.—To dream of seeing a number of fishes of
a choice kind, and delicious to eat, indicates that
you will have much pleasure in all your engagements; you will be comparatively independent. If
you dream that a fish eludes your grasp, slipping
from your fingers; it betokens loss of situation, of
friends, and especially of a lover.

FLEAS.—To dream that you are annoyed by them
indicates harm from evil and malicious enemies;
trade will decrease; friends prove false, and lovers
deceitful.

FLOODS.—For seafaring persons, merchants, &c. to
dream of floods is a favourable dream, denoting successful trade, and a safe voyage, but to ordinary
persons, it denotes bad health, law-suits terminating
unfavourably; also very malignant enemies, proving
injurious. If you are a lover, your rival will, like a
flood, sweep away from your embrace the object of
your affections.

FLOWERS.—To dream that you are gathering
beautiful and fragrant flowers, it is an indication of
prosperity; you will be very fortunate in all you
undertake. If in your dream, you bind the flowers

into a bouquet, it portends your very agreeable marriage. If the bouquet gets loose, and the flowers appear to be scattered, your brightest prospects, and most sanguine hopes will be blasted. If you dream of withered flowers, it portends failing health, and approaching death.

FLYING.—To dream of flying denotes that you will escape many difficulties and dangers. It denotes success in trade and in love. Very likely you will have to travel. If you dream that you are trying to fly very high, it is an indication that you will aspire after a position which you will never reach, and for an office, for which you are not qualified.

FOG.—It denotes great uncertainty. You wish to be accepted as a lover. It is doubtful. You have applied to your friends for assistance. They will never give it. You are speculating in shares, policies, they may ruin you. You are hoping to recover your health. It is contingent. The dream is bad. If you dream that the fog clears away and the sun shines, your state will be happily reversed—uncertainty will banish.

FORTUNE.—It is a dream of contrary. If you dream that one has left you a fortune, it is a sign that he will not. If you dream that your friend has got a fortune, it is a sign of his coming poverty. It is a bad dream.

FOUNTAIN.—To dream you see a muddy fountain indicates trouble. To see a crystal overflowing fountain, denotes abundance, freedom from want. You will be highly respected and honoured. The person whom you love will love you, and your love will be permanent.

FOWLS.—To dream of fowls denotes moderate comfort in temporal things; but in love, it denotes you will meet with slander and rivalry. Be on your guard.

FOX.—If you dream of a fox, you have a sly, lurking enemy—a competitor in trade determined to undermine your interests; and in love a rival determined to displace you. If you are engaged in a law-suit, your counsel is playing two parts, and you will be cast in the end.

FRAUD.—If you charge some one with committing a fraud, you will discover that you have been robbed, and the person who has robbed you. To dream that you have committed a fraud is a dream of contrary, denoting the public appreciation of your character of integrity and honour. If a lover, you will discover the covert acts of your rival, and gain the victory.

FRIENDS.—Dreaming alarmingly of a distant friend, is a sign that sickness, or some evil has befallen that friend. If your dream of distant friends be calm and pleasing, expect good news soon. Your lover will soon return, whose visits will be agreeable, and end in matrimony. Dreaming you see distant friends rejoicing, denotes prosperity to them and to yourself. If they weep the dream is bad. To dream you see a friend dead is a sign of marriage, and *vice versa*.

FRIGHTENED.—To dream that you are terrified at some object, or through any other cause, is a dream of contrary. Terror implies bliss; fright, joy; pain, pleasure. Your bargains, contracts, &c. will be successful. If you dream that you overcome your fears, there will be a glorious turn in your affairs, and you will swim on the tide of prosperity. And, O thou restless lover, all thy fears will be turned into pleasures. It shows that your engagement will end satisfactorily, only persevere and be not daunted by present appearances, however unfavourable they may seem.

FROGS.—Frogs are harmless creatures. To dream of them is favourable; it denotes success in business; to the farmer propitious season, and good crops, and healthy profitable cattle. To all classes, to young and old, it is a good dream, denoting good friends, and public patronage and support. To the lover it is a happy portent :—

> He or she who dreams of frogs,
>   Most certainly shall find,
> Maiden sweet, or swain most dear,
>   Each suited to the mind:
> A wedding gay is coming soon,
> Then, O then, for the honey-moon.

FROST.—This dream denotes very severe trials and troubles. If a female dreams it she is in danger of conquest through a deceitful sensual man, who will eventually desert her. To the man of commerce, it indicates great difficulties in trade.

FRUIT.—To dream of fruit has a different interpretation according to what the fruit is that you dream of. But to dream of a collection of numerous and varied fruits, both English and Foreign, portends unbounded acquisition of wealth—and an agreeable and wealthy matrimonial alliance—a numerous and happy family. The different fruits have different prognostications, thus:

Almonds foretell difficulties, loss of liberty, and deceit in love; bad weather to the sailor, and want of success to the tradesman.

Apples betoken long life and success, a boy to a woman with child, faithfulness in your sweetheart, and riches by trade.

Apricots denote health and prosperity, a speedy marriage, dutiful children, and success in love.

Cherries indicate disappointment in love, vexation in the married state, and slight in love.

Currants prefigure happiness in life, success in undertakings, constancy in your sweetheart, handsome children to the married, and riches to the farmer and tradesman.

Elderberries augur content and riches; to a maiden they bespeak a speedy marriage; to a married woman, that she will shortly be with child; to the tradesman success in business; to the farmer, good crops.

Figs are the forerunners of prosperity and happiness; to the lover they denote the accomplishment of your wishes; to the tradesman increase of trade; they are also indicative of a legacy.

Filberts forbode much trouble and anger from friends; to the tradesman they denote a prison, and decay of trade; to the lover a complete disappointment; to the married, care and undutiful children.

Gooseberries indicate many children, chiefly sons, and an accomplishment of your present pursuits; to the sailor they declare dangers in his next voyage; to the maiden a roving husband; and to the man a rakish wife.

Grapes foretell to the maiden that her husband will be a cheerful companion, and a great songster; they denote much happiness in marriage, and success in trade; if you are in love, they augur a speedy union between you and your sweetheart.

Lemons denote contentions in your family and uneasiness on account of children; they announce the death of some relation, and disappointment in love.

Medlars are a very good omen, they bespeak riches to the dreamer; that you will overcome your enemies, and if you have a lawsuit, you will surely gain it; to the lover they foretell a good husband or wife, with beautiful children and much happiness.

Melons announce speedy recovery to those who are sick; they are indicative of harmony, and inform you that you will speedily accommodate a dispute between you and others; in love, they announce constancy; and in marriage a partner of a happy temper, with handsome children.

Mulberries are of good import; to the maiden they foretell a speedy and happy marriage; to the lover constancy and affection in his mistress; they also denote wealth, honours, and many children; they are particularly favourable to sailors and farmers.

Nuts, if you see clusters of them, denote riches and happiness; to the lover success and a good-tempered sweetheart; if you are gathering of them, it is not a good omen, for you will pursue some matter that will not turn out to your advantage; if you crack them, the person who courts you, or to whom you pay your addresses, will treat you with indifference, and be very unfaithful.

Oranges are very bad omens; they forbode loss of goods and reputation, attacks from thieves, wounds and sickness in the object of your affections.

Peaches are very favourable to the dreamer; if you are in love, they foretell that your love is returned, that you will marry, have many fine children, and be very happy; they denote riches to the tradesman, good crops to the farmer, and a prosperous voyage to the sailor.

GALA.—To dream that you are at a fête or gala, indicates that you will be so circumstanced in life as to be able to enjoy yourself in travel to distant places. If you dream your lover is with you, it portends great conjugal happiness.

GALLOWS.—"This is a very strange dream," says the ancient philosopher, Philater. "It is a dream of contrary. I have known persons come to me and tell this dream to whom I have always said, you will be lucky in all ways; much trade—much money—much honour, a high position. And to the lover I have said, Wishes consummated — hearts tied fast — hands united — happy wedlock — blessed children! Happy lover !"

GAME.—To dream that you are playing at a game, and win, is a sign that you will be very unsuccessful. But if in your dream you appear to lose, it denotes you will be prosperous. If you love one, you will obtain that person as your partner for life.

GAME.—If you see game in the woods, and shoot it, it is a sign that you will obtain the heart you covet. If you dream of abundance of dead game, it denotes a marriage. If the game is decomposing, it denotes the decay of health, and trade. You will be disappointed in love.

GARDEN.—This is a very fortunate dream. Old Ptolemy calls it one of the best. Franximus says,

" I have interpreted many dreams; this among the rest; and have always proved it to be really good. After it I have seen persons rise and become independent of leaky friends—I have seen merchants successful, sailors have a pleasant voyage, farmers have weighty crops, and lovers crowning themselves with rosebuds. All who dream this must rise to wealth and honour." But observe the dream must be of a garden full of shrubs, flowers, and fruit.

GARTER.—To dream that you lose your garter denotes that your circumstance in life will be adverse and uncomfortable. If you dream that your lover picks it up, and gives it you, it denotes the sincerity of purpose, and strength of affection; if your lover gives it you not, you will find that lover a deceiver; should you be united, woe unto you!

GATHER.—To dream of gathering up money is a sign that your state will greatly improve. To gather fruit in season denotes great enjoyment, health, and happiness; but if out of season, it is grief without reason. It betokens enemies, and deceitful love. To dream you gather flowers, denotes that you will marry early and well, and that children, like olive-plants, will be round about your table.

GHOST.—To dream you see a ghost, and the sight appals you, is a very bad omen. Difficulties will come upon you of an overwhelming character. Malignant enemies will try to injure you. But if you are bold in your dream, and see the ghost vanish, it denotes that you will overcome all.

GIANT.—"There is a great difficulty to be encountered, if you have this dream," says Zanchius. "But meet it with pluck and decidedness of soul, and it will vanish. There again, thou dreamest of a giant; well,

it means a knave of an enemy whom thou must encounter.   Beware of his dexterous baits — meet him
fairly in the face—confront him boldly, and thy giant
foe will skulk into *Lethe*."

GLASS.—To dream that you look clearly through
glass, denotes the successful, and even tenor of your
way.   If it is dim and not transparent, it denotes that
your affairs, and your prospects, are very uncertain;
you will be in straits and difficulties.   If you dream
you cannot see at all through the glass, your state
will be decided.   "It denotes," says Fravellus, "when
a lover sees obscure glass, a mutable lover, and an
inconstant friend.   I never knew much luck come
after this dream, and I have interpreted multitudes."

GLOVES.—To dream that you lose your gloves
denotes loss in business, and loss in trade, a change
of abode awaits you; if you dream that you lose
your right hand glove, if married, you will lose your
partner; if single, another will deprive you of your
lover.

GOATS.—You will have enemies, and many trials
through deceit; but your mind will be happy under
all; your trials will not sink you, but operate for
your good.   And you had better be happy in adversity than miserable in luxury and splendour.

GOD.—This is a dream which seldom occurs; it is
principally confined to those who are afflicted, and
those about to die.   It is always a token of death;
except in conversation, when it denotes the prospect
of obtaining mercy, and elevation to usefulness and
honour.   To the pious it denotes a happy death.

GOLD.—"To dream of gold," says Ptolemy, "is a
dream of contrary.   It is a sign of poverty and

distress. Let the tradesman, the merchant, and the adventurer be careful how they place their capital; their speculations will be hazardous. Beware of speculations; it is not all gold that glitters. So with regard to love. To dream that thy lover has plenty of gold, denotes disagreement, when thou marriest thy lover. I fear it will be a sorry wedding. Gold is often an omen of sickness, sorrow, as the results of bad fortune."

GOOSE.—This is a bad dream, for a single man. The woman whom he loves will prove a very silly incompetent wife; she will be a regular gossip, never at peace with her neighbours, and always censuring and quarreling with her husband and his relations. He had better surrender her to some one else.

GOOSEBERRIES.—See *Fruit*.

GRAIN.—To dream that you see a quantity of grain is a most fortunate omen, it implies that by industry and perseverance you will become wealthy and be greatly respected and honoured. To the farmer it denotes favourable seasons, and good crops. If you are in love you will secure the heart of your lover, and have a numerous and happy family.

GRAPES.—See *Fruit*.

GRASS.—To dream that you see green grass, it is an omen that denotes great and continued prosperity; if you dream of withered and decayed grass, the dream is a sign of sickness and distress, and probably an indication to one whom you love.

GRAVE.—To dream of an opened grave is a sign of the dissolution of some near friend or relative. If you dream it under a severe illness, your recovery is doubtful.

GUN.—To dream that you hear the report of a gun, forbodes that you will hear of the death of a distant friend or relative; it also portends that you will be slandered very much by your enemies. But like the report of a gun, that opposition will soon pass away. If the lover dreams of hearing a gun, it denotes a rival determined to supplant you, or to revenge you. It also denotes bad luck to a tradesman, he will have losses through fraudulent debtors.

HAIL.—To dream that it is hailing or snowing, is a bad dream. It denotes disappointed hopes, and blighted prospects. To the farmer unpropitious seasons, and poor crops. To the lover unsuccessful application. To persons in trade heavy losses. Even friends will disappoint your expectations. Are your hopes fixed on your children? Alas! they will not realize those hopes.

HAIR.—If you dream that you have luxuriant hair, it denotes continued health and prosperity. If you dream that your hair is falling off, to a man it is the portent of bad trade; to the husband the omen of an afflicted wife, and vice versa; to the lover the death of his intended. If you dream that your hair turns gray, it is a sign of failing health, of a decaying business, and the decline of a lover's affection.

HAMMER.—To dream that you hear the sound of a hammer, denotes a brisk trade, and great gain. To the operative it is a sign of full employment, and good wages, and of good health, to enjoy the same. To a maiden it prognosticates an agreeable husband, who will ever be industrious, frugal, temperate, and decided to make her life happy, very likely too he will rise in the world, elevate himself, and his family also.

HAMS.—To dream of hams is good. It denotes health and plenty. You will be very happy in the domestic circle ; will love and be beloved.

HANDCUFFS.—A bad dream, denoting that if you are not watchful over your propensities, you will fall into temptation and crime, for which you will have to suffer very severely. There is a bad prospect before you. Awake, therefore that you may not be so degraded. If a lover dreams of being handcuffed to another person, it denotes miserable matrimony.

HANDS.—Dreaming that your hands are tied, denotes difficulties from which it will be difficult to extricate yourself. To dream you are shaking hands with a person, denotes reconciliation after disagreement, or the welcome arrival of some absent friend. To dream your hands are dirty, you are in danger of perpetrating some dishonourable action, or to commence some enterprise which may be unsuccessful and degrade, and distress you. Take warning.

HANGING.—To dream that you are being hung, denotes good to you. You will rise in society, be patronised and wealthy. To dream that you see a person hanged, is an omen of good to him. He also will attain wealth, and great honour.

HARES.—To dream that you see a hare pursued by dogs, is not a good sign ; it portends enemies ; but you will be able to escape. To dream you see a few hares, denotes choice and faithful friends. If a hare runs towards you, it denotes the visit of a dear friend. To a swain or maiden, it is the portent of an early and happy marriage.

HARMONY.—To dream that you hear musical sounds floating in the air, or that you listen to harmony of any kind, is the portent of a long and happy life. In love it denotes that your lover is most amiable and affectionate, and sincerely attached to you. Marriage to you will be a happy boon. This dream is a good omen for all classes.

HARVEST.—To dream of harvest time, and that you see the reapers in the corn field reaping the corn and binding it in sheaves, or that you see the jocund reapers, and hear them shouting, " Harvest home !" is a most favourable dream. You could not have had a better. It denotes prosperity to the farmer especially, many customers for the tradesman, a safe and prosperous voyage to the mariner, and lucrative bargains to the merchant. If a lover dreams of harvest, it prognosticates the consummation of his or her wishes, in early wedlock, happy society, and a numerous and happy offspring.

HAT.—To dream you have a new hat portends success in any scheme. To dream that you lose your hat, or that another takes it off your head, you have an enemy not far off who will both openly and secretly seek your injury. To dream some one puts your hat on his head, it foreshows a rival ; he will supplant you, or it denotes that some one is possessing property which certainly belongs to you.

HEAVEN.—To dream of heaven denotes a change of worlds, and that if you regard your dream, the remnant of your life will be spiritually happy, and your death peaceful. Do not forget this significant dream.

HEDGES.—To dream of green hedges is a sign of agreeable circumstances. If the hedges are flowery, it betokens great prosperity, and success in love. If you cannot pass on your way for thorny briery hedges, it denotes that in business, you will suffer by competitions, and in love, by determined and malignant rivals.

HELL.—This dream forbodes bodily suffering and mental agony, arising from restless enemies, loss in trade, bereavements, &c.

HERBS.—Different herbs are portentous according to their different natures, and medical virtues. Hemlock, Henbane, Aconite, and any poisonous herb, denotes you are surrounded with dangers. To dream of useful and fragrant herbs is good; it denotes agreeable circumstances. Sage denotes honour and advancement, the result of wisdom and prudence. Thyme portends to the lover a happy marriage, and to others, prosperity. Balm denotes sickness, but sure recovery; Horehound a chronic and incurable disease; Wormwood, bitter trials, and overwhelming disappointments. It is bad for the lover. To dream you are gathering herbs, and they are scarce, is a bad omen; if they abound, and are fragrant, it is a very good dream.

HERMIT.—If you dream that you have become a hermit and retired from the world, it indicates that you will have failures in trade, be reduced in your circumstances, and experience great mental depression, but that eventually you will rouse yourself, and surmount every conflict and difficulty, and become wealthy; but to the young it denotes that their marriage is an uncertainty.

HILLS.—To dream of ascending a high steep hill and you are unable to arrive at the top, it is a sign that you will have to labour and toil all your life, and have many difficulties and troubles, and will never be wealthy. It denotes that the lover will never marry, though he or she may approximate to it; something will occur to prevent matrimony. There is many a slip between the cup and the lip.

HOME.—To dream of the home of your childhood, and the scenes of your action in it, in company with your former play-fellows, indicates your continued health and prosperity. To the lover it betokens a true and responsive love, a happy marriage, and great conjugal happiness. You will have a numerous progeny, and each child will do well. To the husbandman, it is a good sign.

HOMICIDE.—To dream of committing this dreadful crime, is an evil dream, it portends many severe misfortunes and heavy losses. "I have frequently seen," says Etius Flaccius," most direful accidents follow this dream, robbery, fire, and death. Art thou a lover? Death will deprive thee of thy object. Art thou a merchant? Loss, loss, will be thine. Dost thou till the ground? Failing crops, diseased cattle, will be thy portion. O man, or, O woman, thy dream is bad indeed, you will be stained by some dreadful crime, and not escape law's penalty. O mother, thy embryo child will be a bad one, overbearing, dishonest, profligate, tyrannical, and degraded."

HONEY.—To dream you are eating honey denotes good health, long life, prosperity and great enjoyment. Your business will be all you can wish, lucrative, raising you to independance. It denotes that your lover is virtuous, sincere, and very fond of you. It would be death to part from you. It denotes that the husband, or the wife, will be of a sweet disposition, industrious, frugal, affectionate and faithful. In fact, as Ptolemy says, " It is a notable dream, foretelling sweetness in wedlock, in the domestic and social circle, and sweetness in all secular pursuits."

HORN.—To dream you hear the sound of a horn denotes intelligence from an absent friend in a distant country, though not of an agreeable nature. If you hear the sound repeatedly, it is a sign of disagreements, and even of war.

HORSE. — Dreaming of this noble animal is generally good. To dream that you are riding a handsome and good horse betokens future independance and happiness. But if it throws you, it denotes that your purposes will be thwarted. If you dream that horsemen approach you, it foretells that you will receive news from a distant friend. To dream of white horses, denotes a marriage, yours, if you are riding upon it. A black horse denotes death.

HOUNDS.—To dream of following the hounds indicates that your pursuits will not be very productive —that your conjugal affiance will disappoint you.

HOUSE.—To dream you build a house, foretells prosperity and success in trade. After such a dream, you may expect a great increase, with better profits. If a sailor dreams of building a house, it foretells a prosperous voyage, and that on his return, he will marry a wealthy woman, and will not go to sea again, except for pleasure.

HUMMING BIRDS.—This dream denotes travel to a foreign clime, and great success in business, or profession there. If you dream of a large flock of humming-birds, it foretells that you will be very fortunate and save money; if you see one dead, you will not succeed, but return to your own country.

HUNTING.—To dream that you hunt a stag, and capture it, is a right good sign of secular prosperity —to the lover, a sign that he will obtain his wish. To dream of hunting a hare denotes misfortune and trouble, and especially disappointment in love. To dream that you are hunting a fox, denotes wily competitors or rivals; if you kill him, it portends your triumph after severe contention.

HUNGER.—To dream that you are very hungry denotes that by your genius and industry you will rise in the world to wealth and honour; to the lover, that your sweetheart will undertake a journey before you marry; in business, prosperity.

HURRICANE.—"This dream I hate," says Tinea Ballater, the Arabian dream explainer, "for it always foreshadows evil. Danger to the traveller and sailot, and disappointment to the dearest lovers. It augurs ill for the trader, and the merchant, and it is the precursor of family feuds and quarrels."

HURT.—To dream of having hurt yourself, or that some one has hurt you, is a dream of contrary, implies that your projects will succeed whether as a lover or a person in business; and that all the malicious attempts of your enemies will prove abortive.

HUSBAND.—To dream you have one, is a dream of contrary; your wish will not be granted. To dream you fall in love with another woman's husband, indicates loose desires, and disregard to virtue. But for a widow to dream that she has a husband, and that he smiles upon her, indicates that she will soon have an offer, and it will be accepted.

HUSBANDRY.—To dream of the implements of husbandry, has a variety of interpretations. To dream of a plough denotes success in life, and a good marriage. To dream of a yoke is unfavourable, unless it be broken, — then it denotes a rising above your present condition. To dream of a scythe shows injury from enemies, and disappointment in love. To dream of a team, denotes death in the family of the dreamer; a sweetheart of very bad temper, and want of success in your undertakings.

HYMEN.—To dream of the god of matrimony, foretells speedy marriage with the person whom you love, and that the union will be very happy and be productive of a numerous family of boys and girls who will rise to eminence, and will do well in the world, and marry rich persons from some distant place.

HYMNS.—To dream of singing hymns indicates a devotional spirit, predicting much happiness, prosperity, and success to the dreamer. The lover will be fortunate, your loved one will be everything that could be desired, and very affectionate.

ICE.—Dreaming of ice is always bad. It foretells failure in trade, unsuccessful speculation and enterprise. It indicates that your now ardent lover is about to cool down and jilt you. To the sailor, it denotes disasters at sea. It is a bad dream for the farmer auguring devastation of crops.

ICICLES.—If you dream you see icicles suspended betokens good luck. If a man he will shortly marry a virgin of great beauty and accomplishments, who will be very much attached to him. They will have a large family of girls, who will have their mother's beauty and marry rich men. To a young woman it predicts a marriage with a man of wealth, and they will have a large family of boys, who will rise to eminence.

IDIOT.—This is a dream of contrary. It indicates that you transact business, and have friendships that you will receive advantages from, or marry an intelligent person. To dream that you are an idiot, foretells your competency for every future engagement.

ILL.—To dream that you are labouring under any illness, denotes that you are in danger of falling into a great temptation, which, if you do not resist, will injure your character. If you are not circumspect, your rival will supplant you.

ILLUMINATION.—Dreaming of an illumination, denotes some joyful occasion at hand. It generally denotes good fortune. In love, you will obtain your wish. In wedlock it is the omen of successful childbirth. Have you no lover? One is coming. Are you about to travel? You will travel successfully. Are you speculating? The prize is yours. Have you a law-suit? The decision will be in your favour. "This is a happy dream," says M. Bonar, "and I have always seen it followed by good."

IMPS.—This dream betokens great grief and vexation. The persons around you will very much annoy you. It indicates false and malicious, and revengeful persons, as your debtors or creditors, as the case may be. The lover is treading on dangerous ground, and trusting in a broken reed; and if he or she continues to trust it may lead to a broken heart.

IMPRISONMENT. — "It is a dream of contrary," says Dr. Sibly. "It prognosticates liberty in every sense, free enjoyment in all states, especially in wedlock."

INFANCY.—If a married woman dreams of infancy, it indicates a peculiar state. To dream of your own infancy, denotes good fortune in trade or profession, or in courtship and matrimonial affairs. To dream you are an infant again is bad.

INDIGENCE.—To dream that you are in indigent circumstances is a good omen, it denotes the receipt of a large sum of money, and is generally the fore-runner of a fortunate occurance. If a woman *enceinte* dreams of being in poverty it foretells she will have a son who will become a great man, marry a foreign lady, and become very rich.

INFIRMARY.—To dream that you are in an infirm-ary, denotes an accident or sickness. To dream you leave it, is a sign of recovery. To dream that you are visiting the patients there foreshows an elevation in your position, and a feeling and generous heart.

INJURY.—To dream that some person or persons have injured you, denotes enemies who have evil designs against you. Beware of them. Walk circum-spectly, and they will not succeed, though they will expose their malicious purposes. If a tradesman, your competitors will conspire against you, and you may sustain losses. To the farmer, such a dream predicts failure of crops by unpropitious seasons of fire. If you are a lover, then the friends of your intended are against you. Take care; you are so surrounded by foes and difficulties that a change of locality is desirable.

INK.—To dream that you are using ink denotes prosperity in business; if you spill it, and dirty your hands, it denotes that your correspondence will not be successful, whether in trade, or in love. You must expect an unfavourable answer.

INN.—It is unlucky to dream of being at an Inn, it denotes poverty and want of success in yonr undertakings; it is the forerunner of sickness, and sometimes death; it sometimes portends poverty, and imprisonment. To the tradesman it denotes loss of money, and a falling off in business. If you are in love, it portends that your sweetheart will jilt you and marry another.

INSANE.—"I have known very sensible and rational men," says Dr. Sibly, "dream that they were insane, and it has always proved a good dream, followed by good health, domestic happiness, rare social enjoyment, and long life. As to the lover, it shows extraordinary affection, decision of purpose, and entire consecration to the person loved."

INSTRUCTION.—To dream that you are receiving instruction, prognosticates that you will shortly be placed in circumstances as to need the advice and assistance of your friends, and it will be well if they come to your relief. To the lover, it indicates a dangerous rival, under which rivalry, you will need help and consolation. Let not jealousy foster revenge. To dream that you give instruction, denotes that your friends will be placed in a similar state, and will require your counsel and aid.

INSULT.—To dream that a person insults you, denotes that you will lose your lover through a silly and trifling quarrel. It also portends that what occurs will go in opposition to your wishes and interests, and that you will be very unfortunate for some time after your dream, unless you rouse yourself, and change your place of residence.

INTEMPERANCE.—To dream of being intemperate in either eating or drinking, foretells sickness and trouble. If a female dreams she sees a drunken man, it is a sign that her husband or lover, is defective in principle, and it will be well for her to renounce him. For a man to dream of an intemperate female, it predicts that his future wife will be a slattern, improvident, and probably drunken. If you see the intemperate party weeping, it denotes permanent virtue and happiness in association.

ISLAND.—To dream that you are on a desolate island implies the death of your lover. If it appears a fertile island, covered with vegetation it implies that your present lover will prove unfaithful; but you will soon meet with a more favourable match.

ITCH.—To dream of having the itch is an unlucky dream, denoting much difficulty and trouble in business and love, you will marry a person of irritable and restless disposition, you are likely to be in adverse circumstances, and very unhappy.

IVORY.—M. Dupone, the French astrologer, says. " This is a superior dream; to the lover it portends beauty, sweetness, virtue, and rare enjoyment. A young female told me this dream; she was poor; but I soon saw her riding in her own coach, with a smart rich man, as her husband. This dream portends abundance to the farmer, success to the merchant, and a safe and prosperous voyage to the sailor.

> Delighted may the maiden be,
> Whene'er she dreams of ivory;
> A rare good sign 'tis sure to prove
> Of fathful and abiding love,
> With one well-suited to her mind,
> A husband tender, loving, kind;
> Rich in estate, they will be one,
> Loving at first they will love on;

The marriage-bond be crown'd with joys,
And round their table girls and boys ;—
Yea, all this bliss is sure to be
To those who dream of ivory!

IVY.—To dream of ivy is a sign that your friend, your lover, your husband, or wife, will adhere to you as ivy clings to the wall. You will have good health and live long. Your enemies will be powerless ; you may smile at them defiantly. In trade, your customers will be constant and abiding. Happy maiden! Happy swain! true love is for you. You will be blessed in your house and store. To the husbandman, it foretells good and lucrative produce, and to sea-faring men, a safe and profitable voyage.

JACKAL.—This dream indicates that you have an inveterate, deep, and sly enemy who will leave no stone unturned to do you an injury, but much to his grief and vexation it will turn out for your advantage. While he falls you will rise ; while he is disappointed, you will triumph. The crafty will be taken in their own snares. To dream that a jackal bites you, it implies you will be much annoyed by a rival who will triumph over your undecided lover. But your loss will turn out a happy one ; though you may grieve at first.

JAIL.—To dream that you are in jail is a dream of contrary. Prosperity in business, freedom from embarrassment, and domestic happiness will be your lot. Quineas Philatus says, that if a virgin dreams that her lover is in jail, it is a sign that she has found an abiding lodgement in the heart of her lover, and will rest there till death do them separate. If a young man dreams that he is in jail, it is a sign that he will succeed in life, and marry the lady of

his choice, the loss of whom he has had reason to
fear. He will ever live as the idol of her heart.
This is also a good dream for a widow. To dream
of escaping from jail, denotes to the person in distress, a favourable change in his circumstances. The
day of adversity will depart. It also indicates the
recovery of health.

JAUNDICE.—To dream that you have the jaundice,
is a bad dream, sickness, or poverty, or disagreements are at hand. If you dream, that your lover
has got the jaundice, it indicates that he or she will
soon discover their real character, which will cause
them to sink in your estimation. Mere pretenders,
hollow-hearted you will find them. To dream that
your wife or husband has the jaundice, is not a good
sign of their fidelity to you.

JACKDAW.—To dream that one crosses your path
is a sign of bitter enemies, who will endeavour to
blast your reputation, and injure you in your affairs.
To dream that you catch a jackdaw is a sign that
you will be able to defy them while they can do you
no harm. It is not a good dream for persons, in
religious society; it indicates opposition from some
of their own sect. It is not a good dream for a
farmer; it denotes indifferent crops.

JEALOUSY.—To dream that you are jealous of
your husband or wife, or sweetheart, as the case
may be, is indicative of trouble and great anxiety.
If you are in business, you may expect your affairs
to be very much agitated and interrupted from unforeseen causes, you will also experience many disappointments in money affairs, and trouble and
annoyance on account of the failure of some with
whom you do business, and also on account of

returned bills. To dream that another is jealous of you, expect misunderstandings, distrust and altered affection. But do not despair it will be all the better for you.

JEWELS.—It is always a good dream, the harbinger of great prosperity, and a great amount of wealth. To dream your lover gives you jewels, it is a sign that his affection is real, and that he will certainly marry you. If a young man dreams that he sees his loved one adorned with jewels, and that he is ravished with the scene, it foretells his speedy and happy union ; that his bride will possess a sweet and lovely disposition. To dream that both you and your lover are counting and inspecting jewels, denotes a numerous and healthy, and fortunate offspring. This dream is good for the merchant, the sailor, and the farmer.

JEWS.—It is a good dream to dream of a Jew, or Jews. It denotes the accumulation of wealth. To a lover, it denotes a speedy and fortunate marriage. It also denotes travel to foreign countries, and successful enterprise there.

JOURNEY.—If you dream that you have to go a journey to some distant country, foretells a great change in your circumstances. If the journey is pleasant such will be the change in your circumstances. If rough, and unpleasant, it is an unfavourable sign.

JOY.—This dream is a sign of good health, and that you will receive a sum of money, or become rich through the inheritance of an unexpected legacy from a distant relative.

JUDGE.—To dream that you stand before a Judge,

indicates that you will be involved in some dispute, or have some serious charges made against you. It is a dream of contrary; for if you dream that the Judge acquits you, it indicates your discomfiture; if he condemns you, it augurs that your plea will be successful, and you will triumph over your enemies.

JUMPING.—To dream that you jump, augurs that you will meet with many impediments and trials; but by industry, courage, and perseverance, you will eventually surmount them. If a single person, it also implies that you will have a sweetheart much attached to you, but whose parents will oppose your union.

KEEPSAKE.—To dream that a friend or lover gives you a keepsake, it implies that some unexpected good will soon be possessed by you; that your friends are anxious for your welfare, and will do all they can to promote it. To a young man it denotes that his future wife will be rich in virtue, and beautiful in person, and will ever be affectionate and constant. To a young woman, it portends that your future husband will be gentlemanly, rich, and renowned, you will have many children, the pledges of your mutual love. To dream that you give keepsakes to others implies your future ability to do so, and you will move in circles of amiable and agreeable friends. But if a keepsake is asked of you, and you are unable to give it, it betokens further poverty and embarrassment, and much sickness.

KERNEL.—To dream of a good kernel, portends favourable circumstances. To dream of an unsound rotten kernel denotes that you will discover a false friend.

KEY.—To dream that you lose a key, denotes disappointment and displeasure. To dream you give a key denotes a marriage ; to find or receive one, the birth of a child ; to dream of many keys, denotes riches, as the result of a flourishing trade.

KILL.—To dream you see a person killing any fowl, bird, or animal, portends that your lover will place his affections on another, and will desert you. To a married woman it announces that some false friend of her husband will make improper advances to her.

KING.—To dream of being in the presence of monarchy, and that you speak to a sovereign, indicates that you will rise to honour and dignity in your country. If the monarch is unfriendly, the dream is unfavourable, and all your expectations will be blasted. If a maiden dreams that she is in company with a king, it foretells that her future husband will be well off, and probably occupy a situation under government.

KISS.—To dream of kissing one whom you should not, is a bad sign ; it denotes a false friend, or a false lover. To see another kiss your intended, portends a rival. To see your lover kiss another person, denotes false love from a false heart. To dream that your lover kisses you with affection, and repeatedly, shows that lover to be true to you, and that his intentions are pure. For married persons to dream of kissing each other, portends that you will meet with an unfaithful companion.

KITE.—To dream you see a kite flying high, portends elevation in your station in life. If you are flying it yourself successfully, and if it flies high and steadily, it is a good sign. You are sure to rise above your present position to dignity and honour; some high official station will be yours. In love it is a good dream, especially for a widow. It frequently foretells travel in distant countries. The farmer may expect large crops,—the sailor a safe and prosperous voyage, and commercial men, a good trade. But if the string should break, and the kite be blown away, it is as bad a dream as you can have. All your enchanting prospects will be blasted.

KITTEN.—To dream that you are playing with a kitten, and that it scratches or bites you, denotes that your sweetheart has a trifling mind, and is of a spiteful disposition, and that if you marry you will have a very unhappy life, and wish yourself single again.

KNAVE (*at cards.*)—To dream of playing at cards, and that you continually hold the knave of diamonds in your hand portends seduction. The knave of hearts, you will meet with a lover; the knave of spades early widowhood and the knave of clubs debt and imprisonment.

KNIFE.—This is a very unfavourable dream. If you see knives cleaned ready for a feast, it is by contrary sign, a portent of poverty. If you see them bright and sharp, it denotes your enemies, and their evil designs against you. If you have a lawsuit pending, it is sure to terminate against you. If you are married, your partner will prove false to you; and if you are a lover, the loved one will reject you and marry another. You will have many disappointments and losses in trade; many ill-willed competitors.

LACE.—If a young man dreams that his sweetheart is adorned with lace, it shows to him that she will be very extravagant and improvident, and unfit to manage a house. She will be a regular dolly.

LADDER.—Brennius Salustis says, "This dream has great import. Art thou young and dreamest that thou hast reached the top of the ladder, thou hast a bright prospect before thee, and thou shalt attain it. Thou shalt kiss in wedlock thy coveted bride, or thy longed-for bridegroom. Man of commerce, it speaks well for thee. The breezes of fortune will blow thee into the harbour of independance. It is the portent of wealth, honour and human glory. Thou tiller of the ground, dost thou dream of reaching the top of the ladder? Thy grounds will bring forth plentifully, and make thee rich. Scholar, student, collegian, up, up, you will reach the climax of your ambition. And thou poor widow, thou, if thou dreamest this, shalt light thy coal again, and thy sorrow shall be turned into joy, but if when thou gettest to the top, and lookest down, and it maketh thee dizzy, it shows that thou wilt not be able to bear preferment; it will make thee proud and arrogant, and thou wilt tumble back into thy former hole of obscurity, Or if the ladder should break as thou goest up, thy hopes will be shipwrecked."

LAKE.—To dream of sailing on a smooth glassy lake, denotes future comfortable circumstances—a happy, pleasing life. It denotes success in business, and all honourable employments. It portends a large but agreeable family. It shows that the lover will be successful, and safely glide into agreeable matrimony. But if the water of the lake appears thick and muddy, it is indicative of much trouble and suffering arising from losses, insolvencies, &c.

LAMBS.—It is always favourable to dream of lambs.

If it be a young woman that dreams, it foretells her that her future husband will be of a sprightly, active disposition, very happy; that she will have many children, who will be healthy, and rise up to honour. If a young man it shows that his future wife will be young, very beautiful and virtuous, but rather inexperienced, and artless, and will need much experience to make her a good housewife. To those who are married, it shows that they will be happy in their children, though they will not escape the attacks of disease.

LAME.—To dream that you are lame implies that your future life will be one of difficulties and disappointments, and that your means of subsistence will be very limited and precarious. Your life will indeed be a warfare.

LAMENT.—To dream that you are lamenting any loss in trade, or by death, is a dream of contrary, you will have cause to rejoice on account of the acquisition [of some property, or the good conduct of your children. To dream that you hear others lamenting denotes good luck to your friends or relatives and that you will rejoice with them. I apprehend too that it is the precursor of a wedding.

LAMPS.—If you dream that you are carrying a bright lamp, it foretells that in your particular calling you will succeed, and be highly esteemed. To the lover it is a good omen. If you dream that you carry a lamp with a dim flickering light, it denotes your sickness; if the light goes out as you carry it, it portends your death, or, at least, the failure of your plans and hopes. To the lover it implies the death of love in the beloved. To dream of seeing many bright lamps denotes a coming festivity. If you appear to be exultant on the occasion, it denotes your marriage.

LAND.—To dream that you possess land is a good dream. It is indicative of wealth and independence. To dream that you give notice to quit land, foretells change of residence, probably in a far country. If you dream that you receive a notice to quit, it betokens reduced circumstances.

LARK.—It is very lucky to dream that you hear the singing of a lark. It denotes good health and prosperity. If not married it shows that your future partner will be rich, and that you will live in the country, and will have many children who will be virtuous, and a credit to you while you live. In all probability, some of your children will be talented musicians and vocalists.

LAUGHING.—To dream that you are laughing immoderately denotes vexation and disappointment. If you are in love it is a certain sign that you will not be reciprocated. The affection of your lover is not decided; it oscillates between you and another. Therefore be cautious how you act. Curb the passion of love; you are likely to be jilted. Laughing is often a sign of weeping and sorrow.

LAUREL.—To dream of Laurel, betokens victory and pleasure. If you marry it foretells possessions by your wife. It foreshows great prosperity. If a woman dreams of it and smells it, it denotes that she will bear children; to a maid, it shows speedy marriage.

LAW.—If you dream that you have a lawsuit, a suit in chancery, or any other case of litigation, it prognosticates very heavy losses in business, and

many great difficulties; after such a dream it will
be very hazardous to enter into any partnership,
compact, security, or bond with any person. Be
careful not to lend money, not to make any purchase immediately after such a dream, or you will
have cause to regret your incautiousness.

LEAD.—To dream of lead denotes many troubles
and quarrels. If in love there will be contention
between you and your lover. If married it denotes
that the affections of your partner are on the decline.
It also foretells family quarrels, and separation, and
great discomfort. It foretells to the sailor, or to a
person about to take a voyage, that they will have
a stormy voyage, that they will suffer shipwreck, and
have a narrow escape from drowning.

LEAVES.—Dreaming you see the trees covered with
beautiful fresh leaves, is good. Your affairs will
prosper. You will succeed in business. It is a rare
good dream for the lover, indicating full and continued affection. If you dream you see blossoms, and
then fruit among the leaves, it denotes your marriage,
and a numerous progeny. If the leaves appeared
withered, ready to fall off, it is not a good omen; it
portends losses in trade, bad crops to the farmer,
disappointments in love, loss of friends by unfaithfulness, or death.

LEARNING.—To dream of being in a place of
learning shows that you will attain influence and
respect by your future diligence. It is a good omen
to dream that you are learning, and easily acquire
knowledge.

LEAPING.—If you dream of leaping over any impediment, it denotes that you will easily surmount

every obstacle to advancement, and eventually rise to honour and affluence. Persevere, and the victory is sure. To persons in love, it shows many impediments and dangers, and also rivals; but if you dream that you leap over any obstacle, it foretells that you will win those whom you love, and be happy.

LEASE.—To dream of taking a house, shop, warehouse, or any other building on lease, foretells great success in trade, and that you will soon live together in marriage with the object of your affections.

LEECH.—To dream you see leeches applied denotes sickness. To dream one bites you, foretells that you will be greatly injured by some one.

LEG.—To dream you have bruised, dislocated, or broken your leg, or lost the use of it, foretells that a young woman will marry a man of intemperate and indolent habits, and who, through his improvident and unsteady conduct, will be always in poverty. It shows to a young man that he will marry a tenderhearted female, but rather irritable, and not a good manager in house affairs.

LEGACY.—The old astrologers declare this to be a lucky dream, always prognosticating the reception of some good fortune. The lovers' union will be a happy one; secular pursuits will be successful; farming occupations, and sea-faring engagements will prosper.

LEMONS.—To dream you see lemons growing on a tree denotes that you will visit a foreign land, and probably marry a native of it. To dream that you eat lemons denotes you will be attacked by a dangerous disease, from which it will be well if you recover. To dream you see a great number of lemons, denotes that your marriage, though pleasant for a while, will greatly disappoint your expectations.

LENDING.—This is not a good dream. You will be surrounded by a good many needy dependants, and by them annoyed, if not, impoverished. It is the omen of losses and great poverty.

LEOPARD. — To dream of these beautiful, yet savage creatures, indicates travel to a foreign land, where you will have to encounter many dangers and difficulties. But you will eventually overcome them, marry well, and be very prosperous and happy. It is likely that you will stay there all your life.

LEPROSY.—To dream that you have the leprosy, is always the forerunner of great troubles and misfortunes. It may also imply that you have been guilty of some crime tending to sorrow and disgrace, and probably imprisonment. You will have many enemies, some of whom will be very near to you.

LETTER.—Dreaming of receiving a letter sometimes indicates presents, or at least the reception of unexpected news, from a person you have not heard of for many years. To dream that you send a letter, denotes that you will soon be able to perform a generous action.

LICE.—This dream foretells much sickness, poverty and tribulation. Yourself, or some one to whom you are tenderly attached will meet with severe affliction, also expect much trouble in your business; it will fall off considerably, or if you are a servant, or manual labourer, it is probable you will lose your situation. This dream frequently prognosticates imprisonment for debt.

LIGHT.—To dream you see a light, of a brilliant

nature, denotes riches and honour; if you see it suddenly extinguished, it denotes a reversion in your affairs.

LIGHTNING.—It is a favourable dream, for it augurs success in business and advancement to honour and independence. To the farmer it portends propitious seasons, and abundant, and well-harvested crops. It is a good dream for the sailor; it foretells fair winds and a quick voyage. To those in love it denotes constancy in affection, and a speedy and happy marriage. If the lightning be attended with storm, rain, hail, and thunder, the dream is a bad one.

LILY.—To dream you see this lovely flower, it is a sign that by your virtuous and industrious career, you will be very happy and prosperous. To the lover it denotes the virtue of the object beloved. The lily is the emblem of purity; therefore it augurs well. If you marry, you will be happy, and have lovely children. If in your dream, you see the lily wither, then your most ardent expectations will be nullified. It portends failure, the death of a lover, a partner, a child, &c.

LINEN.—To dream that you are dressed in clean white linen, denotes that you will shortly receive some good tidings; that your intended is faithful and sincere, and will soon bring matters to a point. It is an omen of great success in business, and of large crops to the farmer, and of domestic felicity. If your linen appears in your dream to be chequered, you are likely to have a legacy left you. If it appears to be dirty, it is the omen of poverty, sickness, wretchedness, and want; also disappointment in love, rivalry, jealousy, &c.

LION.—This dream denotes greatness, future elevation. You will occupy some important and honourable position. To a young woman it foretells that she will be married to a man of noble bearing, superior intellect, and amiable disposition. To a young man, it denotes that his future wife will be no waster, but intellectual, of great spirit, and efficient in household affairs. She will be a help-meet for him indeed.

LIQUORS.—To dream that you drink brandy, is a certain sign that you will emigrate to, and reside in a foreign land, in improved circumstances. If you dream that you drink rum, it portends that you are to be a "sailor's bride," or the bride of one who obtains his livelihood by shipping. If you dream that you drink gin, it foretells that you will live in a large and populous town, and there be the subject of poverty and debt; it foretells great trade losses, and also the loss of your character. Dreaming of drinking whisky prognosticates a sudden reversion in your circumstances, loss of valuable friendships, and the world's scorn of you. You will need more than human support.

LIVERY SERVANTS.—To dream of livery servants, portends that you will soon emerge from your present obscurity, and associate with the wealthy and influential, for which you will be qualified by your possession of wealth. In matters of love it foretells that you will marry a person of independent circumstances, in whose affectionate esteem, you will be very happy indeed.

LOCK.—To dream of locks implies that difficulties will hinder your success. If you see cabinets, drawers, &c., with locks and no keys, it is a bad dream for the tradesman, and for the lover. You cannot effect your object. Your hope is sweet but it will never ripen into fruition. Should you dream that you find keys which open the locks, that circumstance completed, changes the omen of your dream. You will succeed—you will acquire—you will rise. Young woman, or young man, the heart of your lover is in captivity to you. It cannot swerve. Cherish it lovingly therefore.

LOOKING-GLASS.—To dream that you look at yourself in a mirror, indicates that your business is not conducted on sound principles, and must ultimately fail, if you do not properly arrange it. It indicates also that you are surrounded with deceitful persons, whom you will soon discover. In trying to injure you, they unmask themselves. Do not be too confiding, nor be led away by flattery. While you are not suspicious, by rather discriminating. Try to discover motives. And thou who lovest, beware of that rival; he is determined to supplant thee, and it is very likely he will succeed; he will soon show the cloven-foot, though now thou art fascinated by his sugared words to thee.

LOCOMOTIVE.—To dream of a railway-engine, foretells travel, or the arrival of some dear friend.

LOAD.—To dream that you are carrying a heavy load, under which you groan and tremble, foretells that your future life will be one of care and toil. Great difficulties will encompass your paths, many obstructions to your happiness. But if in your dream you are able to carry your load, and carry it to the appointed place safely, then it augurs, you will rise above all your difficulties and troubles, and pass the rest of your days in ease and comfort.

LOTTERY.—To dream of being in a lottery is a

dream of warning to young persons, cautioning them not to be precipitate in giving their hearts to an apparent lover, they are sure to meet with disappointment and vexations. After such a dream, a female ought to consult her friends on the prospects of marriage, and be guided by their advice. A young man ought to be very careful on whom he sets his affections, for this dream foretells that he will be tempted to form an attachment to a female who will render him very unhappy, for she will be overbearing, unamiable, a great scold, fond of drink, and addicted to gossip, and spreading scandalous reports. How true is the addage, "Marriage is a lottery with more blanks than prizes."

LOVE.—To dream that you see *Cupid*, the god of love, and that he smites you with his arrow, is a sign that some one loves you, who will soon declare himself; and the same dream denotes the same to a young man. To dream you do not succeed in love is a dream of contrary ; you will succeed, and marry, and be happy. To dream that your friends love you, foretells future prosperity in business, and great domestic happiness. To dream of being in company with your lover is a good dream. You will soon marry the object of your choice, have many children, who will be to you a source of comfort and joy. To a woman with child it foretells a safe delivery of a lovely child. To dream of loving and being loved, denotes that you will enjoy a large circle of loving friends ready to assist you in any emergency, and be faithful at all times. It foretells to the farmer propitious seasons, heavy crops and much wealth. The sailor will have several good voyages, in the last of which he will marry a rich female, and become settled in life.

LUCKY.—To dream that you are lucky is a dream of contrary. It is the omen of disappointment, and misfortune. After such a dream, be cautious, and keep your eyes open. Let judgment, and not your passions, rule.

LUGGAGE.—If you dream that you are travelling, and that you are encumbered and annoyed with a great deal of heavy luggage, it foretells great trials and difficulties which will cause you much trouble and expense. This will almost overwhelm you, and you will be in great straits, principally caused by embarrassment, or insolvency of others, or the injustice and bad treatment of some of your relatives. To a lover it denotes the delicate health of a future wife or husband, which will be a source of great expense. To a traveller, it foretells danger and disaster.

LUMBER.—To dream that you are surrounded and annoyed with lumber, foretells misfortune and trouble. To dream that you are searching among lumber, and find something valuable, foretells the acquisition of a fortune, which will completely reverse your circumstances.

LUTE.—To dream that you hear the sweet tones of a lute, foretells the receipt of good news from a long absent friend, or from one whom you ardently love. It also denotes to the lover that the person beloved is true, of amiable and engaging manners, and great sweetness of disposition. To a young woman it shows that her lover is devotedly attached to her, and is good tempered, sincere, and constant, but not very rich. They will marry, and have lovely children who will do well, and be their solace in the time of old age. Such a dream foretells a happy old age and good health; and in all cases it is the fore-runner of success and happiness.

LUXURY.—To dream of living in great luxury is a sign of sickness and poverty, and that you will meet with many disappointments. You are not likely to be successful in trade; you will have many crosses, great losses, and be in danger of imprisonment for debt. In love it denotes rivalry, jealousy, and quarrels, between lovers, and to them that are married it foretells disobedient and refractory children, and much family strife and contention.

MACHINERY.—To dream that you are inspecting machinery, and it affords you pleasure, foretells that your trade will prosper, and that you will have to extend your operations to supply the demands of your customers. And thus you will rapidly grow rich, and be honoured by those around you. To a female who dreams that she sees her future husband among machinery, shows that her lover is of industrious habits, and although not now rich, he will ultimately become so.

MACKEREL.—To dream that you see these fishes in the water very clearly, foretells success in trade, prosperity and good fortune. If you dream of stinking mackerel you will never marry your present sweetheart, for she will prove worthless, being false-hearted.

MADNESS.—To dream you are mad, or in company with mad persons, portends well for the dreamer; even vigour of intellect, great efficiency in commercial transactions and adequate remuneration, even to the acquisition of wealth. The merchant, the tradesman, the sea-captain, the farmer, after such a dream may expect an uncommon tide of prosperity. It also betokens good health and long life. "Young persons have asked me about this dream," says old Ptolemy, "and I have invariably told them it was a good ominous dream. Young man, you will find a maiden just to your mind, and right happy in wedlock shalt thou be. Young woman, thy future husband shall be all that thou canst wish; intelligent, wise, industrious, persevering, loving, and ready to die for thee. And all my interpretations have been correct."

MAGIC.—Dreaming of magic foretells changes and revolutions. Some change will take place in your circumstances, but it will be a change for the better. Like magic your present poverty and wretchedness will disappear, and your throbbing heart will be at rest soon. But it indicates also that your hitherto trusted friend will be unmasked by acts of treachery and injustice, but you will triumph over that enemy. Your present love, and that of your sweetheart, will abide only a little longer. Both of you wish for a change. Quick, pass, begone! it is better to be so; and so you will think by and by.

MAGISTRATE.—To dream that you stand charged with crime before a magistrate, it is bad, if he convict you; if he pronounces you free, the dream is ominous of good. If you dream that you are raised to the magistracy, it foretells future advancement to a high official station, with great honour, and large emoluments.

MAGNET.—To dream that you see a number of magnets foretells that your path will be laid with snares; mind you are not ensnared with such fascinations. If you dream that you are using a magnet, it indicates that you are plotting and planning against some one to bring them under your power for selfish purposes. If you see others using the magnet, and you see your lover near, depend upon it you have rivals, who will leave no stone unturned to get you into their power. Beware of such. If a maiden sees her lover using a magnet it portends the hollowness of his heart, his language to be insincere, and all his vows, and sighs, and declarations, to be utterly worthless. His intentions are quite dishonourable, therefore shun such company.

MAGPIE.—To dream that you see a magpie, fore-tells that you will soon be married, but that you will lose your partner in a few years after your union, To dream you see two magpies, it denotes that you will be married twice, and be twice widowed. And if a man dreams that he sees three magpies, it portends the death of his wife in childbed, and also the death of the child.

MALT.—To dream that you are brewing malt into beer is a sign of marriage, and much domestic enjoy-ment. To dream that you see a large quantity of malt in a maltkiln, and purchase it, is the omen of great prosperity, and of long life, and a comfortable old age. If a female dreams of malt it is likely that she will marry a publican who will become a great drunkard. If a woman with child dreams of malt, the child will be a male, and he will grow up to be a drunkard.

MANNA.—To dream of manna is rather a fortunate dream, denoting that though the journey of life will be chequered, yet there will be many comforts to sweeten its bitters; there will be light in darkness, and the conquest of every difficulty.

MANSLAUGHTER.—To dream that you have been

guilty of manslaughter, foretells misunderstandings, family jars and quarrels. You will disagree with a very intimate friend. It also denotes rivalry in love, and very angry, if not violent contentions, and the separation of lovers. It foretells losses in business, and probably insolvency. It is a bad dream predicting robbery, fire, destruction of property and life on land and on sea.

MANUFACTORY.—To dream that you are inspecting a factory, when all is in operation, denotes that your trade will flourish, by which you will acquire much wealth, and be very useful all your life. It also betokens a time of commercial prosperity generally.

MAP.—To dream that you are inspecting a map indicates that you will have to leave your native land and reside many years in a foreign country, but eventually you will return to your own country. If you inspect a plain map you will return poor; but if it be a coloured map, you will come back very wealthy, which will make you happy in old age. If a female inspects a map in her dream, it indicates that her husband and her sons will be great travellers.

MARIGOLDS.—To dream of marigolds denotes a constant lover, and a happy marriage; also elevation in circumstances, accumulation of riches and honours, and great success in your undertakings and constancy in love.

MARINER.—To dream that you are a mariner, intimates that very likely you will have to emigrate to some distant part. To dream you see a number of mariners, portends news from abroad; and to the man of business it indicates successful bargains and seafaring transactions. If a young woman dreams of mariners, and one in particular, it foretells that a sailor will be her husband; if she dreams of a mariner in distress at sea by storms, &c., it is a dream of contrary; her husband will safely return.

MARKET.—To dream that you are in a market, marketing, denotes a good trade, competent circumstances, and high domestic enjoyment. It denotes some approaching happy event, which will be the cause of joy and feasting. If a female dreams that she is in a market, where many look at her, it is a sign she will have many lovers, and it will be difficult for her to decide which to take.

MARMALADE.—To dream that you are eating marmalade alone, portends personal sickness. If you dream that you are eating it with other persons, it indicates that you will meet with many kind friends who will ever be ready to comfort and cheer you. To dream that you eat marmalade with only one person, portends that the soft speech, and sugared words of your lover are likely to deceive you. Beware of mere pretenders. To dream that you make marmalade, denotes a wedding at which you will be prominent.

MARRIAGE.—To dream you see a marriage is a sign of an interment in which you are interested. To dream you are married is· ominous of death. It is very unfavourable to the dreamer; it denotes poverty, a prison, misfortune, and the alienation of a lover. To dream that you assist at a wedding, portends some pleasing news, indicating advancement in life for you. To the sailor the dream of marriage augurs storms, and shipwrecks, and narrow escape from death.

MARSH.—To dream that you are walking in a marshy country, portends a troubled life. If you can scarcely get along for swamps, it denotes many sorrows and difficulties. But if you get on easily and out of the marsh soon, it foretells that the remnant of your days will be passed in moderate comfort. To the lover this dream shows many scrapes and trials, but ultimate triumph over every impediment and foe.

MARTYR.—To dream of the age of the martyrs denotes that you will be firmly attached to the verities of the Christian religion, and be in intimate alliance with the excellent of the earth. To dream that you are a martyr, is indicative of your unwavering defence of the truth, and your triumph over all hostility.

MASK.—Should a young person dream that his or her lover appears to them wearing a mask, it is a sure sign of insincerity and deceit. It shows double dealing, a pretending of love to you, while engaged to marry another. Learn to discriminate and to ascertain motives.

MASTIFF.—To dream you see a mastiff, is a sure sign that some one whom you suspect of infidelity is, after all, your best friend. If you dream that you are bitten by a mastiff, it prognosticates that some pretended friends will greatly injure you, especially in love affairs ; they will anxiously strive to supplant you in the affections of your sweetheart. If a maid dreams of a mastiff, it shows that her lover is faithful and true.

MAY-POLE.—To dream that you dance round the May-pole, or that you are watching others dance round one, announces the advent of some joyous occasion. It also foretells a long and happy life, that you will never want, but always have a competence ; neither poverty nor riches. It also foretells that a maiden will marry a sober and industrious person, with whom she will be very happy, and by whom she will have a numerous family. Their children will rise up healthy and strong, virtuous and happy, and will not forsake them in time of old age. If a widow dreams of dancing round a May-pole it foretells that she will marry again.

MEADOW.—To dream that you are walking through a meadow, predicts good fortune to you. If a maiden dreams that she is walking with a young man in a meadow, it is a sign that her beau will be very loving, that he will marry her, and acquire riches, and by him she will have a numerous and beautiful family, and will be very happy and live long. To a young man, it denotes that he will marry a beautiful and rich young lady, who will be devotedly attached to him, and be his constant solace. They will have a numerous family characterised by honour and happiness.

MEASLES.—To dream that you are ill of the measles, denotes that riches are about to drop into your lap from a quarter which you did not expect to yield any thing. It also implies returning health, and business prosperity.

MEDICINE.—To dream that you are taking medicine, and it tastes nauseous to the palate, implies that something will occur to you that will be very annoying and unpleasant for a little time only, and then be of much service to you. The dark clouds will vanish, and light appear. Rest will follow toil, and pleasure pain. It is a good dream.

MELONS.—A young man, or a young woman who dreams of melons is destined to marry or be married to a rich foreigner, and to live in a foreign land. Such a union will be crowned with great happiness, be attended with great wealth ; their children will be few, but they will be virtuous and happy.

MENDICANT.—To dream that you are a beggar is a dream of contrary. You will amass wealth, and be far above the reach of poverty. You will marry a person comparatively poor ; but she will be a virtuous woman, whose price is above rubies. To dream that you are accosted in the street by a beggar, denotes great trouble through a seeming friend, who however can do you no harm.

METALS.—To dream of gold denotes great trials, sickness, loss of property, and pecuniary embarrassment. To dream of silver foretells that you will meet with deceitful persons, and disappointment in love. To dream of copper coins, denotes poverty, and to dream of the metal, denotes shipwrecks and accidents during travelling. To dream of iron indicates that you will marry a person of great spirit, and that you will acquire great wealth through your own industry, and successful speculations. To dream of lead portends the loss of your lover or the death of some beloved friend or relation.

MICE.—To dream of mice indicates many intermeddling enemies and slanderers, also poverty and unsuccessful undertakings. It also foretells an unfortunate marriage and disobedient children.

MICROSCOPE.—To dream that you are looking through a microscope, denotes that you will discover some lurking and deceitful enemy, who will appear to you in real character, no longer under a disguise ;

also that you will be separated from your lover by removal to a distance; but you will meet again in happy wedlock, and have a numerous progeny.

MILK.—To dream that you drink milk, foretells joy. To dream of selling milk, denotes bad trade, and disappointments in love. To dream that you give milk, denotes prosperity, and a happy marriage. To dream that you see it flowing from a woman's breast, denotes marriage, and a very large family. To dream of milking a cow, foretells great plenty to the farmer, healthy cattle, and abundant crops.

MIMIC.—To dream you hear a ludicrous imitation, indicates that you will meet with a mere pretender to pecuniary ability; one on whom it would not be safe to depend, or to trust. It portends also that you will have a lover whose intentions respecting you are quite dishonourable. Endeavour, therefore, to find out motives.

MINCE-PIES.—To dream of eating mince-pies intimates that you will have to be at a wedding. To dream that you are making mince-pies, portends that you will soon be making preparations for your marriage. Your partner will be tolerably well off, though not affluent.

MISER.—This is an unfavourable dream. It foretells bad success through life, and great troubles. You will never rise above your present circumstances, but probably become poorer and more wretched. In love it foretells marriage with a person who will make you miserable by low despicable ways, and that you will have many bad children.

MISFORTUNE.—To dream that some misfortune has happened to you or your lover, is a dream of contrary, foretelling that a person will be very fortunate

in business, and have a very happy selection of a lover.
You will rise in life, and be greatly respected and
esteemed. In married life you will be very comfortable ; your children will be numerous, healthy, and a
source of comfort to you.

MONEY.—To dream that you pay money, foretells
your competency to do it through a prosperous business. To dream that you receive money foretells the
birth of a child, or the gain of a law-suit ; it generally portends prosperity. To dream you find money
foretells sudden advancement through a prosperous
business and by marriage.

MOON.—To dream of the moon, foretells unexpected joy, and success in love. If it be a new moon
it is a good dream for the tradesman, and farmer, and
lover. The full moon denotes marriage ; it is good
for a widow.

MOTHS.—To dream of moths indicates enemies, who
are doing you great injury, and labouring to undermine your position in life. It also portends that your
lover will hear reports about you that will cause a
quarrel between you, and probably a separation. To
persons in trade it indicates that you have dishonest
and unfaithful servants who are injuring you in your
business.

MOTHER.—To dream that you see your mother
and converse pleasantly with her, denotes your comfort and prosperity through life. If a female, who
has a lover, dreams that she has become a mother, it
is a sad dream. To dream that you lose your mother,
denotes her sickness.

MOUNTAIN.—To dream that you are ascending a
steep and rugged mountain, shows a life of toil and

sorrow; all your endeavours to better yourself will be thwarted by unforeseen events, as afflictions, losses, &c., and it is to be feared that you will never rise in the world, for calamities will come thick upon you.

MOURNING.—This is a dream of contrary. It portends good concerning you. Your lover is genuine, entirely devoted to you, and is sure to marry you, and to make you very happy. To the married it denotes much comfort, and to the merchant, tradesman, and sea-faring man, it denotes great prosperity. The farmer will reap abundantly.

MURDER.—To dream that you have committed murder, is an awfully portentous dream. It foretells your vicious life, the perpetration of evil, and probably imprisonment. After such a dream, repent and abandon sin and evil associations, or it will be dreadful for you. To the tradesman and farmer, it foretells many grievous losses, by failures and robbery. It denotes that your lover will prove false.

MUSHROOMS. — To dream that you are eating mushrooms denotes personal sickness. To dream that you are gathering them, foretells the accumulation of wealth.

MUSIC.—To dream you hear delicious music is a very favourable omen; it denotes joyful news from a long absent friend; to married people it denotes sweet-tempered children; in love, it shows that your sweetheart is very fond of you. Rough and discordant music denotes trouble and vexation.

MYRTLE.—To dream you see a beautiful and fragrant myrtle, denotes agreeable circumstances. To a young person it foretells a very suitable and agreeable lover, a very pleasant courtship, leading to the altar of Hymen. It portends a legacy to the dreamer. If a married person dreams of a myrtle-tree, it foretells that he or she will be married twice, and the second time to a person who has been married before. Also, you will have a very numerous family, the most of which will live to maturity and grow wealthy.

NAKED.—To dream that you are naked is a bad omen, foretelling poverty, disgrace, and misfortune. If you are engaged in business, it is a sign that you will fail, become bankrupt, and very narrowly escape imprisonment. If you are in the sea-faring line, expect storms, shipwreck, and great sufferings. If you are a farmer, you will have bad crops, and you will lose many of your cattle, and suffer by robbery. To lovers it foretells that they will never marry those whom they now address; but another person of disagreeable temper, arbitrary, selfish, and tyrannical. The imprudence and self-gratification of such a person will inevitably produce ruin. To married persons it foretells infidelity in a partner, great misery, and very disobedient children.

NAME.—To dream that you have changed your name, is a sign that you will never be married.

NECKLACE.—To dream that you are wearing a rich and costly necklace, most surely portends that you will speedily make a conquest of a very wealthy person; the courtship will pleasantly continue, till consummated by happy wedlock. Numerous beautiful children, mostly females, will be the pledges of pure and sincere affection. They will all grow up very beautiful and marry rich men. If a female dreams that she breaks the necklace and loses the beads, her children will die young, and she will become poor in her old age.

NECTAR.—To dream that you are drinking nectar foretells that you will accumulate riches and honour, and that you will rise beyond your most sanguine expectations. It also shows that you will marry a handsome person in high life and live in great state, to an old age.

NEST (*of Birds.*)—Dreaming of a bird's nest, prognosticates marriage and domestic happiness. You will have a comfortable nest with many young ones in it, who will be honourable and creditable to you. To a sailor it foretells that he will find a rich wife and a happy home at the next port he enters; and to the tradesman it presages great success, and consequent independence; to the farmer it predicts a plentiful harvest. If you dream of a bird's nest having broken eggs, or dead birds, it is a bad dream, betokening failure and distress.

NETTLES.—To dream of nettles prognosticates good health, and worldly prosperity; but to dream that you are stung by nettles indicates vexation and disappointment. You will be deeply hurt by the ungrateful conduct of some pretended friend; and if you are in love, your sweetheart will be tempted to deceive you and to marry your rival.

NEWSPAPER.—Dreaming that you are reading a newspaper shows that you will hear from a distant friend good news, which will cause you to quit your present employment, but you will succeed much better for the change. You will be exalted above common servitude, and be able to commence business

on your own account, in which you will have great
success, and amass great riches.   If you are a single
man, it portends that you will marry a widow, and
that you will have an expensive lawsuit which never-
theless will end in your favour.   To persons in love
it shows that the object of their affections will remove to a distant part of the world, and it will be
many years before they are again united, but their
reunion will be a very happy one.   To the politician,
it betokens great and stirring events in the nation.
To the farmer it shows a favourable season and an
advance in the price of grain.   To the sailor a prosperous and quick voyage.

NIGHT.—To dream that night suddenly overtakes
you, denotes a great change in your situation ; a
change from competency to want and dark adversity.
To dream that you are walking on a dark night,
denotes grief and disappointment, losses and misfortunes.   If you are in business, you will have many
losses and bad debts, and probably become insolvent,
and be sent to prison.   If you are a farmer, you will
suffer bad crops and a loss of some of your best
cattle ; and if you are a sailor, it denotes a stormy
voyage and a miserably small freight.   To those who
are in love it foretells some very unpleasant misunderstandings and contentions with your sweetheart
which will most likely end in a separation.   If you
are married, it indicates that your partner is unfaithful to you, and friendly with an intimate friend and
companion.

NIGHTINGALE.—To dream of hearing this sweet-
singing bird, is a very propitious omen, and may
always be regarded as the harbinger of joy, success,
and prosperity.   It is a good dream for persons in

adversity, or for the sick; as it betokens a reverse of their state. It is a sign that a single person will meet with a lover, whose person, manners, intellectual qualities and acquirements, will be very enchanting. The exclamation will be, "How sweet is thy voice, and thy countenance is comely." Young person, you could not have a better dream. You will be admired and be greatly loved. You will be married, and have children; some of them will possess great vocal powers, and all of them will be a comfort to you. To dream that you hear the nightingale indicates that all your undertakings will be successful. Good fortune will await you; probably advancement to some high and lucrative position.

NIGHTMARE.—To dream that you have the nightmare signifies that you are under the influence of a foolish and imprudent person.

NINEPINS.—To dream of playing at this game implies great fluctuation and reverses in business, caused by heavy losses. You will be reduced in your state, and have to struggle with great poverty. It also denotes hollow-hearted friendships, false lovers, and disappointments in love and marriage.

NOISES.—To dream of hearing great and alarming noises foretells domestic quarrels and dissensions; and much misery in consequence. You will be alienated from your best friends and lose the esteem of your relatives. If you are a lover, it portends that through bad influence, your intended will abandon you.

NOSE BLEEDING.—To dream that you are bleeding at the nose, denotes that you will have sickness, and your life be in danger. To persons in trade it denotes bad trade and heavy losses. If you are

engaged in a trial or lawsuit it portends that you
will be cast with expenses, which will almost overwhelm you. If you are in love you may expect that
your lover will prove unfaithful to you and marry
your most intimate friend. It also forebodes contentions and separations in your own family, which
will greatly distress you for a season; but afterwards the breach will be healed, and happiness
return. Such a dream should warn you not to travel
for some time after this dream, as it prognosticates
accidents, nor to enter into any new undertaking;
above all to avoid lending money, or you will lose
both the money and the friendship of those to whom
you lend it.

NOSEGAY.—To dream that a person gives you a
nosegay, shows friendship. If you dream a young
man gives you one, it is a sign that you will have a
very agreeable lover ; If you dream that you give
one to a young woman, it denotes that your addresses will be agreeable, and you will be accepted.

NUISANCE.—To dream you see a nuisance and
that you have to remove it, denotes that your life
will be disagreeable, and one of drudgery. If you
dream that another person has committed a nuisance,
you will soon hear of the disgrace and degradation of
an acquaintance.

NUN.—For a young female to dream that she has
entered a nunnery, and become a nun, prognosticates
disappointment in love, and that she will experience
much sorrow, almost driving her mad. It also warns
her to beware of seduction, and not to put undue confidence in the faith of man. Strive to investigate the
motives which actuate him.

NUTS.—To dream of nuts having good kernels, is

a good omen, denoting that you will become wealthy
through the possession of a good legacy, and that you
will marry an agreeable and rather affluent person,
and rear a numerous and happy family, that you will
live to a good old age, and be highly respected by a
large circle of friends and acquaintances.

OAK.—To dream of a large oak with beautiful foliage is a very good dream. To the man of business
it indicates a steady and permanent trade, and that
you will be able to endure and surmount all trials.
To a family it denotes constant and abiding domestic
happiness. It also forebodes a happy, hale, and robust old age. To a young man it portends that he
will commence business and succeed, and that he will
marry a pretty and intelligent woman, of courageous
and resolute disposition, very efficient in domestic
management, very industrious, and having a very
amiable disposition. To a young woman, it foreshows
that her future husband will be handsome, having a
strong and robust constitution ; he will be very temperate, industrious, and decided for the support and
enjoyment of his family, and especially for their education and moral training. To dream of an oak full
of acorns, foretells of unbounded prosperity. To
dream of a withered and decayed oak indicates that
your brightest prospects will be blasted, while the
latter part of your life will be full of poverty and loss.
A blasted oak foretells sudden death.

OATS.—For a farmer to dream that he sees fine oats
in the fields, or otherwise, it portends a bountiful harvest, and a sunny time for reaping the same. For a
merchant, it augurs successful commercial enterprise ;
and it indicates to the tradesman a flourishing busi-
nass ; to all, that their plans shall succeed. To the

young man about to commence business, it is a good
omen ; he will succeed in gaining a fortune by industry
and perseverance. If intending to travel, it is a favourable omen ; the traveller, and the sailor will have a
safe and lucrative journey. If you are engaged in a
lawsuit with any one, it indicates that the result will
be in your favour. If you are single, and dream that
you are walking with a person through a field of
green oats, it is a sign that your intended is only
simple and inexperienced ; it through a field of ripe
oats, it denotes your intended to have a good intellect, and ardent and sincere intentions. You will soon
be married, and have an interesting family.

OCEAN.—To dream that you gaze upon the ocean
when it is calm, is good ; when it is stormy and tur-
bid, it augurs ill. To dream of sailing on the ocean
when it is smooth, and the weather calm, with favourable breezes, certainly denotes the accomplishment of
a purpose, designs answered, and the object devoutly
wished for, obtained. After such a dream happiness
and satisfaction will follow. It prognosticates success
in love affairs. To lovers, it foreshows that they will
have a delicious courtship, and sail straight and honourably on into the harbour of matrimony. Your
wishes will meet in one another, and you will have
mutual and endearing affection. To the sailor, this is
a dream of contrary, if he dreams of a pleasant voyage, it denotes a stormy and unsuccessful voyage ; if
he dreams of a stormy voyage, it portends the reverse,
a fine, safe, and prosperous voyage.

OFFENCE.—To dream that some one has given you
offence, certainly portends that some disagreeable
altercations will take place between you and your
lover, or between you and your most particular

friend, which will end in cessation of intercourse and friendship, and which will not soon be made up. Beware of giving cause to others for offence, and be very guarded in your speech. If you have opinions of your own, do not try dogmatically to enforce them upon others. In your discussions be mild and persuasive, so that none may have an advantage over you. To dream that you are so offended as to seek revenge, or that an offended person is so disposed, beware, for there is danger that your passions may hurry yon away into difficulties, or that you may receive injury from another.

OFFICE.—To dream you are turned out of your office, foreshows death and loss of property; to a lover it indicates want of affection in your sweetheart, and misery if you marry the present object of your affections; to a sailor, it announces bad weather and shipwreck.

OLD MAN.—For a woman to dream she is courted by an old man, is a sure prognostic that she will receive a sum of money, and be successful in her undertaking. For a maid to dream of it, shows that she will marry a rich young fellow, will have many children by him, who will all become rich.

OLD WOMAN.—For a man to dream he is courting an old woman, and that she returns his love, is a very fortunate omen, it prefigures success in worldly concerns; that he will marry a beautiful young woman, have lovely children, and be very happy.

OLIVES.—To dream that you are gathering olives, denotes peace, delight, and happiness in domestic life, and in every situation. To dream that you are eating olives, it foretells that you will rise above your present circumstances, whatever they may be; that you will obtain the favour and patronage of influential men, who will cause you to fill a profitable government situation and acquire wealth. For a person in love to dream of olives, either gathering or eating them, foretells that the person who addresses you is characterized by cincerity and truth. You will have a happy conjugal life, attended with great prosperity.

ONIONS.—To dream that you are eating onions portends the discovery of a valuable treasure, or lost goods and money. To dream of paring onions and to have your eyes affected thereby, denotes quarrels with your friends, or with your family, which will be deeply affecting to you. To dream that you are getting onions, denotes that a friend will recover from sickness.

ORANGES.—This dream is generally unfavourable. It foretells personal and relative sickness and misfortune; also misunderstandings and family jars. To the lover, dreaming of oranges foretells coldness on the part of your lover, and growing indifference, and ultimate cruel abandonment of you. If you afterwards enter the marriage life, and dream about oranges, it denotes an unhappy marriage. In commerce, it foretells heavy losses through insolvency, and through the dishonesty of those employed. And to the farmer they indicate failure of crops, and other losses.

ORCHARD.—To dream that you are in an orchard, gathering fruit, agreeable to the taste, as well as pleasant to the eye, foretells that you will be made the heir to some property, and become rich. If the fruit appears ripe, your advancement will be immediate; if green, it is yet in the distance; but it will come.

ORGAN.—To dream that you see an organ, and hear it pealing beautiful anthems, &c., in a place of worship, predicts to persons in business great prosperity; to the sailor, a pleasant and prosperous voyage, and to the farmer a bountiful harvest. To persons in love it portends fortunate marriage, with very suitable persons, and children who will rise up to be blessings and ornaments in society.

OVEN.—To dream that you are baking in an oven, foretells moderate success in trade. But if you burn the bread, and it appears black, it portends disaster. Your trade will fail, and for a season, you will fall into poverty. It also denotes jealousy, rivalry, and quarrels among lovers, caused by an envious and undermining female, who is likely to succeed in causing separation.

OVERBOARD.—To dream that you have fallen overboard at sea, denotes sickness, poverty, imprisonment, and bad success in your undertakings. It also forewarns you that some friend, or perhaps your lover, will turn perfidious, act a strange deceitful part, and by duplicity and misrepresentations, cause you great grief and sorrow. You will be in danger of sinking under the trial; but you will eventually surmount it, and be happy in a true lover. To a farmer it prognosticates disease amongst his cattle, and his poultry. To the sailor it is a dream of contrary, foretelling a safe voyage to a distant part, and a safe arrival at home.

OWL.—To dream that you see this bird of night, and that you hear it howl, denotes sickness, poverty, and disgrace. After dreaming of an owl, never expect to meet with continued prosperity, or to marry

your present lover, or to succeed in your present
undertakings.

OX.—To dream that you see a herd of oxen is the
harbinger of great prosperity and success in your
engagements, particularly if you see them grazing, in
which case it denotes the accumulation of immense
wealth, and your elevation to honour and dignity.
To lovers, it presages a happy and fortunate marriage, and that your partner will have a legacy left
by a wealthy relative. To dream that you are pursued by an ox foretells that you will have an enemy
or rival, who will much annoy you.

OYSTERS.—To dream of eating oysters foretells
that after many conflicts, and heavy losses, you will
acquire wealth and independance; that married persons shall enjoy domestic happiness, and that lovers
by patiently waiting, shall obtain their wish by a
happy conjugal alliance.

PAIN.—This is a dream of contrary. If you dream
that you suffer great pain denotes the advent of
some particular event, by which you will be greatly
benefited. To persons in trade it foretells that there
will be a great advance in the prices of some of the
goods which they sell, by which advance they will
realize considerable profits. To lovers it is an omen
for good, foretelling the arrival of the propitious time
when they will realize with partners possessing an
ample fortune. To the farmer it foretells a very con-
genial and rich season, and that he will obtain a
greater price for his product than ever he did; and
to the sailor it prognosticates that he will marry a
rich widow at the next port he touches at.

PALACE.—To dream that you live in a palace is a
good omen, foreshowing that you will emerge from

your present obscurity, and be elevated to a state of wealth and dignity. To the lover it portends an agreeable partner, and a very happy marriage.

PALM-TREE.—To dream that you see a palm-tree in full blossom, and smell its fragrance, is a very significant dream, in which case it predicts much success, prosperity and happiness to the dreamer, particularly in matters of love. Notwithstanding your fears and misgivings you will secure the affections of your lover never more to be alienated from you; your love so mutual, shall be crowned with union at the altar. Children, the sweet pledges of your affection will gather around your table like olive-plants, and they will grow up to be useful and honoured while they live. It also foretells successful speculations, a flourishing trade; deliverance from pecuniary difficulties, and the fortunate result of a lawsuit, a ripe old age, and much comfort to it.

PANCAKES.—To dream that you are eating pancakes denotes the fruition of hope, the arrival of some joyous occasion, that you have long been expecting. In matters of love it foretells that you will be shortly married, and that your partner will be loving, industrious, and frugal, and study to make you very happy. If you are trying to turn a pancake, and cannot succeed, it bespeaks loss in business, and failure in love.

PANTOMIME.—To dream that you witness a pantomime at a theatre, implies that you live among deceitful persons; and that those who profess to be your friends, and flatter you, and speak well to your face, are deceitful in heart, and are labouring insiduously to injure you as much as they can. You will soon find them out, as in reference to business and love matters, they will shortly develop their real characters.

PAPER OR PARCHMENT.—To dream of paper or parchment implies that you will get into trouble, and most likely you will be accused of some crime that will cost a deal of money and anxiety before you can exculpate yourself. To dream that you can see clean paper, denotes that the affection of your friend or lover is unquestionably sincere. To dream of dirty, scribbled, or blotted paper shows the reverse; also unjust and dirty actions. If the paper is properly written on, it portends good bargains. If folded up, or crushed, it denotes disappointments; if neatly folded, that you will obtain your wish.

PARADISE.—This is certainly a good dream, denoting to married persons, a religious and happy life, patient endurance of all its sorrows, a bright hope of immortality, and, after the cessation of life, a sure and certain entrance into Paradise. To a young man, it foretells that his wife will be a virtuous woman, will have some property, will have many interesting children, and will be a help-meet for him in every sense. To a young woman, it foreshows that her husband will be an intellectual man, pious, and very indefatigable in business, and to produce domestic comfort. She will have very beautiful, healthy, and interesting children. They will be very good and obedient, and rise to eminency. This is a good dream for the farmer; portending abundant crops, and a glorious harvest. It is a good dream for the emigrant, denoting that the country in which he has decided to live will meet all his expectations, and that he will be very happy and prosperous there. To every one who dreams about Paradise, it is the omen of good.

PARCEL.—To dream that you receive a parcel denotes good fortune. You will either hear from a friend, or receive a present; if you dream that you are carrying a parcel through the streets, it denotes great changes in business, and a loss of custom, and greatly reduced circumstances. It also denotes disappointment in love matters, and that your lover will marry another person. If a lover dreams of receiving a parcel, it is a favourable omen, denoting success in love.

PARK.—To dream of walking through a park, indicates health and happiness, and true friendship. To a person in trade it is the harbinger of a flourishing business. If you dream that you have the company of another person with you, it denotes a true and faithful lover, and a speedy marriage. The now apparent obstacles will all vanish. Such a dream is very good for a scholar, or a person seeking perferment. It is also a propitious dream for the merchant, sailor, and farmer.

PARLIAMENT.—To dream that you are a member of the house of parliament, foretells advancement. To dream that you are only a visitor, and that you listen to the debates, foretells family quarrels and dissensions; also that you will quarrel with your sweetheart and friends.

PARROTS.—To dream you hear a parrot talk, foretells that you will have a very talkative person for your companion. To dream that you see many parrots foretells that you will emigrate to a foreign country, where you will settle and marry, and be very happy. You will cultivate land and by it amass great wealth, and secure great dignity and honour. You will only have two children, a boy and a girl; the latter will be married to a rich man ; and the former will become an official character, and be very useful and highly esteemed.

PARTRIDGE.—To dream that you see a flock or covey of partridges, foretells many troubles and misfortunes ; but if they fly away, it portends that you will overcome them all and be happy. Partridges also denote enemies and false friends who will endeavour to create prejudices against you, and to sow dissensions between you and your lover.

PASSING-BELL.—To dream that you hear the solemn knell of the passing bell, portends personal or relative sickness ; also misfortunes and great trouble. It also denotes your bereavement of a parent, or relative, or friend. It is not a favourable dream for a lover, as it denotes that he or she will not marry their present lover, but will have to mourn on account of his or her death. It portends no good fortune to the tradesman, nor to the farmer, nor to the sailor. Your present schemes will not be successful. In law, if you do abandon the lawsuit, you are sure to fail.

PATH.—Walking in a good path denotes success in trade, in farming, and in love matters ; if married, it denotes that a female will have a safe delivery, and that the whole family will be happy. If, in your dream, the path appears crooked, and filled occasionally with thorns, it foretells disappointments and treacherous friends.

PAWNBROKER.—To dream of being at a pawnbroker's pawning any article, foretells losses, misfortunes, troubles, and disappointments. It portends that you will have some quarrel or dispute with some person that will end in a trial or lawsuit, which will go against you, and nearly plunge you into ruin. If

you are a lover it foretells that your sweetheart is
unfaithful to you and prefers another, and that they
will be married, to your great chagrin ; but despond
not ; the loss will be your gain, as you will some-
time 'after be allied to a superior person. If you
are after any office, situation, or appointment, this
dream foretells that you will be an unsuccessful
candidate.

PEACHES.—To dream that you are eating peaches,
foretells personal sickness, which though very severe,
will soon pass away, and you will be healthy and
strong again. To dream that you see peaches growing,
denotes deceit in love and friendship.

PEACOCK.—To dream that you see a Peacock with
its feathers spread, denotes an unsound and uncertain
position in life, and that you are surrounded with
seeming friends, but who are deceitful. If you see
the bird with its feathers not spread, it foretells a
young man that he will marry a beautiful wife, and
attain riches and honour ; and that a female will
marry a handsome man, and live in ease and comfort,
but she will have no children. To the farmer it denotes a favourable harvest ; and to the sailor that he
will marry a rich widow.

PEARS.—To dream of pears prognosticates great
wealth, and that you will be considerably elevated
above your present situation to one of dignity and
emolument. For a female to dream of pears, denotes
that she will marry a person far above her rank, and
she will live in splendour and happiness, notwithstanding her past ignoble condition. To persons in
trade, this dream denotes success, the accumulation
of wealth, and independency. It also foretells constancy in love and happiness in the marriage state.

PEARLS.—This is a very favourable dream, it foretells to the dreamer that by his own perseverance and industry he will amass great wealth, and arrive at great honours and dignities ; that however poor he may be at the beginning of his business life, he will die a rich and great man, respected by the general public. To dream that pearls are given to you, denotes a marriage with a very beautiful virgin, having an amiable disposition and possessing great accomplishments, who will make him very happy.   If a maiden dreams that some one adorns her with pearls, it foretells her marriage with a very rich man.

PEAS.—This is a good dream.   To dream that you are eating them, denotes great prosperity.   If you dream that you see them growing, it foretells good fortune in love, and a happy marriage.   To dream of dried peas, foretells the acquisition of wealth.

PERJURY.—To dream that you have been guilty of perjury, foretells your future imprudence, and want of conscientiousness, which will expose you to contempt, and subject you to neglect.   This will reverse your state, and reduce you to poverty and straits.   It also foretells sickness, troubles, and losses ; and in love, the unhappy choice of a partner for life ; your children will be a source of annoyance, being refractory and disobedient, and not doing well.   To the sailor it denotes suffering by shipwreck ; and to the farmer very bad crops.

PERFUME.—To dream that you are using a perfume, or that you smell its rich fragrance, is always a favourable dream in reference to business, the seasons, association, &c., and in love matters.

PHANTOM.—To dream that you see a phantom denotes that your expectation of the success of your plans will be disappointed. Appearances may flatter you; but in vain. You think that you have secured the affection of your lover, but a rival will come and supplant you, and your lover will regard you with disdain. O be aware, of the contingency of human passions! It also denotes a quarrel with your best friend, which will cause you much sorrow. It also forebodes danger by travel, and loss of money by lending, and by giving too much credit.

PHEASANTS.—To dream that you see pheasants flying across your path, or in a field or plantation, it foretells that a relative or friend will leave you a legacy. If you dream that you see them fight, and fly away, you will be in danger of losing your legacy by a lawsuit.

PICTURES.—To dream of pictures is not good, it indicates falsehood and deceit. It matters not how beautiful the pictures may appear to you in your dream, it foretells your troubles arising from false and deceitful persons, who will malign your character, and restlessly try to damage your reputation. If you love any one, as your future partner, that person is false, however gracious and loving he or she may be. That person has been attracted by another, and they are only making you a tool to awaken jealousy and an endeavour to restore former intercourse. Therefore, labour, to ascertain *motives*. To persons who are married it foretells the infidelity of their partner.

PIGS.—To dream about pigs is the harbinger of a mixture of good and bad luck; it shows that you will have many false friends, but that you will have a sincere and faithful lover. It implies much sorrow and sickness, and that you will be exposed to great dangers, and especially to the danger of losing your life, but you will escape with a slight injury. It also forebodes that, notwithstanding many obstacles, you will rise in the world, and have a competency of worldly substance. But your children will be unfortunate; by their improvidence they will fall into poverty and disgrace.

PIGEONS.—To dream of seeing pigeons flying in the air or otherwise, prognosticates that you will receive important intelligence; they also denote a happy and suitable partner, and constancy and happiness in love. Also great success in trade, and the acquisition of wealth thereby.

PINE-APPLES.—To dream of pine-apples portends an invitation to a feast or wedding, where you will meet a person you will afterwards marry. You will marry well and happily, and have many fine children who will all grow up rich and respectable. It also foretells great success in business transactions. To the emigrant it bespeaks a safe voyage, and contentment and happiness in the country where he will settle.

PISTOL.—To dream that you hear the report of a pistol, foretells calamity coming upon you. If you dream that you are firing a pistol, it foretells that you will marry a person of hasty and passionate disposition, but very industrious. It also foretells that your marriage will be moderately happy; that you will have many children who will do well in the world; particularly the first-born who is sure to be conspicuous in the world, and be renowned for some great accomplishment or gift of nature.

PIT.—To dream that you are descending a pit shows that your business is rapidly declining, and that you will become the subject of want and distress. To a person in love it indicates the alienation of your lover's heart, and that he will treat you with cold indifference. To dream of falling into a pit, forebodes that you will be involved in misfortunes and troubles, and have many heavy losses; also that your lover or partner is unfaithful to you; and is actually permitting the advances of another lover, who, under the mask of friendship is wounding you in the most sensitive part. To a farmer it foretells bad crops, foul weather, and diseased cattle. After such a dream the merchant must meet with heavy losses, and the sea-faring man with disastrous weather, and terrible storms.

PLAY.—To dream that you are at a play, where you have much amusement betokens happiness in the marriage-state, and extensive success in trade. To a young man, or woman, it portends that they will marry well. To dream that you are taking part in a play, is not a good dream.

PLOUGHING.—For a young woman to dream that she sees a young man ploughing is a good omen, denoting that her future husband will be honest, sober, and industrious; and will by his own efforts and perseverance raise himself to independence. If a young man dreams that he is ploughing in a field, it foretells him that he will become very wealthy through his own exertions and industry. It also indicates much happiness in married life.

PLUMS.—To dream that you are gathering green plums, foretells much sickness in your family. To dream that you are gathering ripe plums in their season is a good dream for all. To dream that you pick them off the ground and they are rotten, denotes false friends, and a deceitful lover, and also a change in position, that you will fall into poverty and disgrace. If you dream that some one gives you ripe plums, and you find them good to eat, it foretells that you will have an agreeable lover, that you will marry, and have a very comfortable home.

POISON.—To dream that you have taken poison foretells a reversion in your circumstances; it denotes that your business will be unremunerating, that you will suffer through the dishonesty of others, and as a consequence be in poverty and distress. If you dream that you recover from the effects of poison, it is a sign that you will extricate yourself from difficulties, and do well. If you dream that another offers you poison, it foretells a treacherous lover, falsehearted, and foul; but, though you will be disappointed in your first lover, you will soon get another very much superior.

PRECIPICE.—To dream that you are on the edge of a precipice is a dream to forewarn you to abandon your present engagements and pursuits, for they are sure to turn out disadvantageously and to your great loss. After such a dream avoid taking a voyage or journey, or you will repent it. Your lover is not trustworthy, and you have seen some indications of it; take warning, and after such a dream, renounce the connection. In trade do not be too confiding; if after such a dream, you trust your goods, or lend your money, you are sure to be imposed upon.

PREGNANCY.—If a married woman dreams that she is pregnant, it implies the birth of twins: and if a young woman dreams the same, it denotes that her sweetheart's motives are not honourable, and that he has a design on her virtue, only wanting to make a meal of her.

PRISON.—To dream that you are in prison is a dream of contrary. It indicates freedom, happiness, unbounded scope in trade. In love, it foretells that you will marry a person whom you have known for a long time, but whom you have not regarded in the light of a lover. To dream that you are putting someone in prison, foretells that you will be invited to the wedding of an acquaintance or relative.

PROVISIONS.—To dream that you are hungry, and require provisions, and cannot obtain them foretells poverty and want. But to dream that you have abundance of provisions stored up implies a future state of competency, and in probability, it foretells a long journey, either by sea or land, and that you will be in many dangers; but that you will overcome them all, and in a foreign land acquire much wealth, and return with your abundance to your native land.

PUBLIC HOUSE.—To dream that you are keeping a public house denotes that you will be driven to extremities in your temporal affairs, and be compelled to act against your inclinations. To dream that you are drinking at a public house, is a bad omen, indicating sickness and poverty, and probably imprisonment for debt. In love it foretells cruel and deceitful treatment by a lover, who will very coolly abandon his attention towards you. In business it foreshows great losses. To sailors it foretells shipwreck and misfortunes; and to the farmer a great loss of crops through bad weather, and loss of cattle through the influence of epidemic disease.

PURSE.—If you dream that you find a full purse, it foreshows great happiness, particularly in love;

and that you will marry a person of great property by whom you will have a numerous family. To dream of losing a purse foretells your own sickness, or that of your lover.

QUADRUPEDS.—To dream that you see many quadrupeds of various kinds, portends that you will pass through a life of toil and labour, but in the end you will accumulate wealth, and be very happy and comfortable in your old age.

QUAILS.—It is an unlucky dream, denoting bad intelligence, and family jars. It also shows that you will lose your lover through false aud artful reports; it also foretells disasters at sea. It also tells you to beware of false and deceitful friends and lovers. It is not an omen of happy matrimony.

QUARRELS.—This is a dream of contrary; for if you dream that you quarrel with some person, it foretells success in business or in love, and that you will enjoy much wealth, and a married life, notwithstanding all opposition.

QUEEN.—To dream that you are in the presence of the queen foretells advancement to a honourable position in life. This will be effected principally by your efforts; also you will have many friends. To a young woman it shows that she will marry a person holding a high official situation in the state, that they will have a numerous family, and become very rich and happy.

QUICKSAND.—To dream that you are walking amongst quicksands, implies that you are surrounded with many temptations, and have many propensities to evil, and you do not know it. It is to be feared that you will run into many dangers through your own imprudence and hasty conduct, and thereby damage your reputation.

QUOITS.—Dreaming that you are playing at quoits indicates uncertainty in trade, and losses, and probably a reverse in your circumstances. It is to be feared that poverty will overtake you.

RABBITS.—To dream that you see rabbits implies that you will soon have to reside in a large and populous city, where you will marry and have a very numerous family. It also foretells that you will have a flourishing trade, that your plans will be successful, and that you will triumph over many enemies. For a married woman to dream of rabbits, indicates increase of family.

RACE.—To dream that you run a race on foot, betokens the defeat of your competitor; it foretells your success in business. You will secure the affections of the one whom you so ardently love. You need not fear a rival, you will marry and be happy.

RAFFLE.—This dream of chance foretells mean associations, and degraded habits. You will sustain the loss of character, the ruin of your business, and meet treacherous people, false love, and disappointment in matrimony.

RAIN.—To dream of rain generally foretells trouble, especially if it be heavy and attended with boisterous winds. To dream of gentle spring rain, is a very good dream, denoting prosperous circumstances, and happy love.

RAINBOW.—This is a token for good. It portends change, but a change for the better.

RATS.—To dream about rats, foretells many enemies who will cause you a great deal of trouble and anxiety, and by whom you will suffer many losses. In love it denotes a rival who has great influence over your intended, and who will leave no stone unturned to supplant you. You are in great danger from such evil designing persons. It is however the best to suffer the loss of a person who is not invulnerable to such specious baits. In matrimony it shows that some pretended friend is studying how to undermine your happiness and peace of mind.

RAVENS.—This is a bad dream. It declares that trouble is coming, that mischief is brewing; you will suffer through injustice, and have to contend with poverty and adversity, and have many sorrows. In love it shows that your lover is false, and your partner is to be suspected.

RICH.—To dream that you are rich is a dream of contrary. You will be poor for a long time; and only gain competency in the end.

RING.—If a married woman dreams that she loses her ring off her finger, it portends the infidelity of her husband, and that he is under the influence of a fallen female, who will ultimately ruin him. If a female dreams that her wedding-ring breaks, it foreshows the death of her husband; and if she dreams it presses her finger and hurts her, it forewarns her of the illness of her husband, or some of the family. To dream some one puts a ring on your finger, foretells union with the person you love.

RIVER.—To dream that you see a broad, rapid, and muddy river and tempestuous, it denotes troubles and difficulties in love and business; but if the river appears calm, with a glassy surface, it foretells great happiness in love, happy wedlock, beautiful children, and commercial prosperity.

ROSES.—To dream of roses in their season is the omen of happiness, prosperity, and long life. If the roses are full and fragrant, it foretells to a young man who dreams it that his mistress will be fair and beautiful, intelligent and amiable, and that their union will follow in due time, and be honourable and happy. It is a good dream for the tradesman and for all, prognosticating great success. If the roses are decayed, it indicates trouble and poverty.

SAILING.—To dream that you are sailing in a ship on smooth water, foretells prosperity ; on a tempestuous sea, misfortunes. To sail to, and arrive at a pleasant country, denotes happiness in wedlock. To dream that you are sailing in a small boat, and that you gain the harbour, it foretells that you will make a rapid fortune.

SERPENT.—This foretells a deadly enemy bent on your ruin. If you are a lover, there is a rival replete with envy and malice, who will labour to displace you from the heart of your lover ; indeed this serpent has already fascinated, and your star is beginning to wane ; you are injured by artful insinuations, and base falsehoods. Let not such treatment destroy your peace and happiness. To dream that you kill a serpent, portends that you will vanquish your enemies and be successful in love, matrimony, and business.

SHAVING.—To dream that a person is shaving you, denotes a treacherous lover ; and great disappointments ; if you are married it denotes infidelity and discord ; and to the man in business, it foretells losses.

SHEAVES.—To dream that you see a field full of sheaves of corn, denotes a favourable harvest, and a

time of plenty. If you dream that you are gathering
the sheaves into your own garner, it is a sign that
you will acquire wealth by your enterprise. If you
see the sheaves fallen down, in a state of confusion,
it predicts a bad harvest, and a time of scarcity.
To dream that you see fine corn in sheaves, and
standing well, denotes to you prosperity, a very
happy marriage, and beautiful, and obedient children.

SHEEP.—To dream you see sheep feeding is a portent of great prosperity and enjoyment. To dream
you see them scattered, denotes that you will meet
with persecution. To see sheep-shearing indicates
riches, by marrying a wealthy person, this will make
you independent of business.

SHIP, OR SHIPS.—To dream that you have a ship
of your own sailing on the sea with merchandise,
foretells your advancement to riches. To dream that
you have taken a berth in a ship, and that you sail
on the ocean, denotes that you will emigrate to a
foreign country, where you will settle for a long time.
To dream you land safely, and walk out with a
person occasionally, it denotes that you will be married to a person in that country; that your union
will be a happy one; you will have children, and
amass great wealth, return to your own country, and
live to a good old age. If you dream that you are
in a ship, and it becomes leaky, it is a sign that
your voyage will not be successful; If a woman enciente dreams about ships, it portends that her offspring will be a male, who will be engaged in a sea-
faring life.

SHIPWRECK.—To dream you suffer shipwreck betokens misfortunes. To a lover great disappointment

in love. Your lover will be reduced in his circumstances, and unable to marry you. To a male it portends that the fair one will fall ill, and perhaps die. To dream that you see others shipwrecked, is a dream of contrary; you will see the elevation of some friends, or relatives.

SHOES.—To dream that you have got a new pair of shoes, is a sign that you will have to take many journeys. If you dream that your shoes hurt you, it denotes that you will be unsuccessful in your engagements. It is a bad sign for a lover. If you dream that your shoes take in water, it shows that you will be calumniated; it portends the falsehood of a lover. To dream that you are without shoes, denotes that you will pass through life with comfort and honour. To the lover it betokens virtue, sincerity, and ardent affection in your intended.

SHOOTING.—To dream that you are shooting a bird, and succeed, is very portentous. It denotes that the tradesman will accomplish his purpose; that the lover will secure the company and marriage with the person desired. But if you dream that you shoot and miss, is a bad portent. It denotes that in business you will be unsuccessful. The dream has the same prognostication to the merchant, the farmer, and the seaman. To dream that you shoot game foretells elevation to a state of wealth, and domestic happiness. To dream that you shoot a bird of prey is a sign that you will conquer your enemies.

SHOP.—To dream that you keep a shop is a sign of moderate comfort. You will have to succeed by industry and perseverance. To dream that you are serving with another person in a shop, indicates that you will meet with a conjugal partner of agreeable mind and manners; and that you will strive together most heartily, and at length succeed in acquiring an independency.

SILK.—To dream that you see silk, or buy, or sell silk, is an omen of good fortune to the tradesman. If the lover dreams of seeing a female in silk, it foreshows that his future wife will be wealthy and very agreeable, being most ardently and sincerely attached to him. If a female dreams she is dressed in silk, it foretells that her future husband will be in good circumstances, and that both will move in respectable society.

SILVER.—To dream that you are collecting small silver coins, foreshows distress; if large coins, you will be engaged in some lucrative trade. To dream that you are paying silver for goods which you receive, or of receiving silver for goods which you sell, denotes a prosperous trade, though but limited. To dream that you possess silver vessels, services, it foretells poverty; you will have to be content with earthenware, if you can get that. To dream that your silver turns out not real, foretells a false friend, or lover.

SINGING.—It is a dream of contrary, and foretells cause for weeping, and lamentation. It is portentous whether you dream you sing yourself, or hear others sing. The tradesman will suffer loss from his customers, the merchant will have no returns for the goods which he has shipped, and the sailor will have a very bad voyage through winds and storms, and the vessel in which he sails will become a wreck. If you love, it portends that the object will cause you to mourn by loving another in preference. To dream that you hear others singing denotes distress amoug your friends and relatives, and that you will suffer through their misfortunes.

SNAKES.—This dream denotes sly and inveterate enemies, who will conspire against you, and by whom you will suffer in your character and estate. It fore-tells that you will have a false lover, who will aban-don you in a heartless manner. To dream that you destroy a snake, denotes that you will vanquish your foes, and all your rivals in love.

SNAILS.—To dream of snails, is not a very good dream. It foretells that you will be annoyed with very low evil-designing persons. Be watchful, lest you suffer through their designs.

SNOW.—To dream that you see the ground covered with snow is a sign of prosperity, and that you will maintain an unblemished character in spite of the attempts of your foes to blacken it. To dream that you are walking upon snow with your intended, fore-tells that your intended will be very beautiful and good. To dream that you are in a snow-storm and very much harassed, is a good dream. You will have difficulties, and calumny; but you will over-come, and come out of the ordeal unscathed.

SOLDIERS.—To dream that you are a soldier, fore-tells that you will abandon your present employment, and change from one thing to another. It is a bad omen for a young woman; she will marry a worth-less man, with whom she will experience much trouble. To the tradesman it prognosticates severe and heavy losses. To dream you see soldiers fight-ing, denotes that you will be concerned in some seri-ous contentions.

SUN.—To dream of seeing the sun foretells suc-

cess in obtaining wealth, and success in love. To
dream that you see it rise, denotes good news; to
see it set, disagreeable news to the tradesman and
losses. To dream that you see the sun overcast, is a
sign of troubles, and great changes.

SWEETHEART.—If you dream that your absent
sweetheart is beautiful and attractive, is a sign of
purity and constancy. If you dream that your
sweetheart is pale and sickly, it is a sign of inconstancy, and probably of falsehood.

TEETH.—To dream that you see a person with
white regular teeth, denotes that you will have a
beautiful lover whom you will marry. To dream
that your teeth are very loose, portends personal
sickness; to dream that one of them comes out, denotes the loss of a friend or relative; to dream that
they all fall out, is a sign of your own death. To
dream that you have the toothache is a dream of
contrary; it denotes much social enjoyment and
pleasure. To dream that you cut a new tooth, denotes change of residence, and to the married an
increase of family.

TEMPEST.—This dream indicates many troubles,
and losses, but you will surmount them; and recover
from them; much persecution, but your enemies can
do you no harm. The lover need not fear rivalry, for
the object beloved is superior to all temptation, however enchanting.

THIEVES.—To dream of thieves, is a bad dream;
it denotes loss in all cases.

THORNS.—To dream of thorns, portends grief, care,
and difficulties.

THUNDER.—To see lightning, and to hear loud

peals of thunder, implies that you will be exposed to hazard and danger, from which faithful friends will extricate you. You should be on your guard after such a dream. If you are pursuing any vicious course, you are, by your dream warned to abandon it immediately, or it will be your ruin. If you dream that you see lightning and hear thunder at a distance, it denotes that you overcome all the enemies and dangers that threatened you, and become very successful in business, and be very rich. All your speculations will be successful. So to the lover; he or she, however jealous and fearful in the past, shall succeed and grasp the prize in happy wedlock.

TOADS.—This dream, to a tradesman, denotes ill-disposed competitors in the same line of business, and determined opposition from them. For a lover to dream of a toad, or toads, foretells that the object of your affection is low and mean, undecided, and inconstant, and not invulnerable to the advances, of a flattering and deceitful person. To dream that you kill a toad, denotes success and triumph in all cases.

TOMBS.—To dream that you are walking among tombs, foretells marriages; to dream that you are ordering your own tomb, denotes that you will shortly be married; but to see that tomb fall into ruins denotes the reverse, and also great sickness and trouble to your family. To dream that you, with another person are admiring tombs, denotes your future partner to be very suitable for you. To dream you are inspecting the tombs of the illustrious dead, denotes your speedy advancement to honour and wealth.

TREES.—To dream you see beautiful trees in rich

and beautiful foliage, and fruit-trees in bloom, or full
of fruit, augurs unusual prosperity in business, in farming, in commercial or maritime affairs.   If a lover
dreams of seeing trees in blossom, or fruit, it is the
portent of a really good marriage, of this worlds
goods, and numerous beautiful and virtuous children.
To dream you see trees cut down intimates the loss
of friends by removal, or death, and also losses in
business.   To dream of climbing trees implies that
your course through this life will be up the hill
difficulty.

TRUMPET.—To dream that you blow a trumpet
is a sign of prosperity, and of the total discomfiture
of your enemies who have striven hard to injure you.
But if you dream that you hear the sound of a trumpet, it denotes coming trouble.   Your competitors in
trade will have the best of the race.   You will have
quarrels in your family, or with your relatives, or
friends.   You will hear of an insolvency which will
tend greatly to embarrass you.   And if thou art a
lover, it is the trumpet of rivalry which thou hast
heard ; thy rival has conquered, and thou wilt soon
know it.

TURKEY.—This is a showy bird, and to dream you
see one, denotes instability in trade, and friendship.
Let not the lover be attracted by gaudy appearance,
for this dream portends union with a vain, irritable,
and bad-tempered person.   Therefore, be on your
guard.

UNFAITHFUL.—To dream that your friend, partner,
or lover, is unfaithful, is a dream of contrary ; they
will be just the reverse.   But to dream that you are
unfaithful, denotes the approach of some peculiar

temptation which may put your profession of attachment to the test.

VAULTS.—To dream of being in vaults, deep cellars, or places under ground, signifies the loss of a lover, and matching with one who has been married before.

VERMIN.—To dream that you are infested with vermin foretells sickness; but if you dream that you get rid of them, restoration to health.

VIOLIN.—To dream that you hear the music of a violin, foretells some social gathering, at which you will be a guest. It may be a marriage, the birth of a child, or the return of a friend from a distant country. To see dancing with the music denotes prosperity; and also the wishes of lovers agreeably consummated in matrimony.

VIPER.—Can this be a good dream? certainly not. It indicates that you have many bad persons around you as enemies, who will strive to injure you. It denotes an unfaithful partner. Your lover is false-hearted, and will sting you yet, by the most disreputable conduct.

VISION.—To dream that you see a person in a vision, prognosticates the sudden and unexpected death of a person appearing to you. To dream you see places, property, valuables, in a vision, denotes disappointment, poverty and misery.

VOICE.—To dream that you hear merry voices, foretells distress and weeping. To dream you hear the voice of lamentation prognosticates cause for joy. To dream that you hear many voices in conversation indicates some joyous event.

VOLCANO.—To dream of a volcano, foretells great disagreements, family jars, and lovers' quarrels. If you are designing to revenge yourself on any one, the injury will fall upon yourself. You will have to rue such a disposition. To a man of commerce, it portends dishonest servants, and a robbery, or some sad convulsion. It also implies civil disorders. To lovers, it is a sign that all deceit, intrigue, base designs, on one side, or the other, will be exploded, and the designer will be branded with the contempt and execration, so justly deserved.

VOLUME.—To dream that you are reading a volume, denotes that you will acquire fame, perhaps literary fame. To open a volume you do not like, and you put it from you, implies insavory associates, and the performance of disagreeable business. If a person in your dream presents you with a volume which you much admire, it foretells an agreeable courtship which will terminate in joyful matrimony.

VOLUNTEER.—To dream that you are a volunteer, denotes that you will be a soldier, and be wounded, or lose your life in battle. For a female to dream that she is walking with a volunteer, is a sign that she will be married to a soldier.

VULTURE.—To dream you see a vulture, is a really bad dream. It is evident that some enemy or enemies are seeking to destroy your character and reputation. Let lovers beware. There is a rival malevolent and decided, determined to possess at all hazards, and determined to revenge.

WAGGON.—To dream that you are driving a waggon, is a sign of poverty; if the vehicle is your own, it foretells advancement. To dream of riding in a waggon portends loss of situation or loss of character and credit. If you dream that a loaded waggon comes to your door, foretells that some one will befriend you, by which you will be advanced in life.

WALLS.—To dream of walls as a barrier, and which you cannot climb, denotes great difficulties in trade, and much embarrassment in family affairs. If you see your lover on the other side of a wall, which you cannot get over, foretells that there will be insuperable difficulties in the way of your union. You will have to encounter the opposition of your lover's friends and parents; besides, the advances of a rival will cause hesitancy and oscillation. To dream that you walk on narrow walls and high, foretells dangerous enterprise; but to descend without injury, or the wall falling, denotes success.

WAR.—This is not a good dream. It foretells to the tradesman, much competition and rivalry in trade. To a family it portends an occurrence which will interrupt domestic peace and happiness. It indicates great mutation in health and in circumstances; poverty frequently following competency, and vice versa, and health often interrupted by sickness. If a female dreams about war, very likely she will be the wife of a soldier; and if a woman enciente dream of wars, it is a sign that her next male child will rise up to become a soldier.

WAREHOUSE.—For you, tradesman, to dream of being in a warehouse, predicts that you will succeed well in business, and obtain large possessions, through your indefatigable labour and exertions. It also foretells that the dreamer will marry a female having a considerable portion, and rear a very interesting family. To a merchant, farmer, and speculator, it is also a good portentous dream.

WEDDING.—To dream of a wedding, portends a funeral near you or among your relatives. To dream that you are married, is a dream of contrary, it denotes a life of single blessedness. For a sick person to dream of being married, foretells his death, and the same applies to a female. To dream that your lover is married to another, foretells that your lover will expose you.

WEEPING.—To dream that you weep is a sign that you will have cause for joy. In trade you will be very fortunate, and when you see the results of your enterprise, trade, or speculation, you will rejoice. You will be crossed in love, perhaps lose your intended; but you will have cause to rejoice in a more amiable and loving friend. Your clouds, even in family trouble, have silver linings eventually.

WHEAT.—To dream that you see a field of ripe wheat, portends that you will grow very rich, and eventually retire independent; that you will marry a rich and very beautiful person, by whom you will have a large family of interesting and intelligent children, who will be your comfort in life's sad decline. It predicts to the sailor that he will have a safe voyage, return home to marry a person of good fortune, which will qualify him to retire from the sea to live in affluence.

WIDOW.—To dream that you are conversing with a widow, foreshows that you will lose your wife by death. For a woman to dream that she is a widow, portends the infidelity of her husband. For a young woman to dream that she has been married, and become a widow, prognosticates that her lover will abandon her.

WIDOWER.—To dream that you are one, denotes the sickness of your wife. For a young woman to dream that she is married to a widower, denotes much trouble with false hearted lovers : but she will be happily married at last to a man of sense and good conduct.

WIFE.—To dream that you are a wife portends you will not be one. For a man to dream he sees his wife, portends her sickness, but she will recover.

WIND.—To dream of a brisk wind, denotes joyful tidings. To dream of strong stormy blasts denotes trouble in all states, and crosses in love.

WINE.—To dream that you are drinking wine, portends health, wealth, long life, and happiness. To dream that you are drinking wine with other persons in great hilarity, foretells your wedding-feast. You will marry the person who has captivated your heart. If you are married, this dream denotes that you will have many children, who will reverence and honour you. If you are in trade you will find it very lucrative, and eventually you will retire independent. This dream also indicates that the troubles of a family will be short in duration, and be followed by high enjoyment.

WREATH.—To dream that you have a wreath upon your head, denotes the conquest of difficulties, and the successful enterprise of trade, to a lover, it denotes union with a superior parson, and great festivities on that account. All will be followed by permanent happiness, except the common ills or infirmities to which poor humanity is always liable.

YEW-TREE.—This dream denotes the death of an aged person, or relation, or patron, from whom you will possess a legacy which will place you above want. If you dream that you sit under a yew-tree, it foretells that your life will not be long. But if you merely gaze upon it, and admire it, it is a sign that you will live long.

YOUNG.—To dream of young persons is a sign of domestic enjoyment. To dream that you were once young, is a sign of your sickness. To dream that you have become young again, is a sign of your approaching dissolution. For young persons in love to dream of their childhood, is the precursor of agreeable courtship, with very loving persons, and ultimate marriage.

THE POPULAR FORTUNE TELLER.

THE POPULAR

FORTUNE TELLER:

CONTAINS

NEVER-FAILING MEANS FOR LADIES TO OBTAIN
GOOD HUSBANDS, AND HUSBANDS GOOD WIVES;

INTERPRETATION OF DREAMS,

FORETELLING FUTURE EVENTS AND
CONTINGENCIES.

ALSO,

THE ART OF DIVINATION,

BY THE SCIENCES OF ASTROLOGY, PHYSIOGNOMY,
PALMISTRY, MOLES, CARDS, &c.

THE SILENT LANGUAGE, &c.

By SIBLY,
THE GREAT ASTROLOGER.

LONDON:
W. NICHOLSON & SONS, LIMITED,
26, PATERNOSTER SQUARE, E.C.,
AND ALBION WORKS, WAKEFIELD.

THE GENERAL FORTUNE TELLER;

OR, BOOK OF FATE.

OF PHYSIOGNOMY.

OF Prognostics to be drawn from the Colour and Nature of the Hair of Men and Women—as also from the Forehead, Eyebrows, Eyes, Nose, Mouth, Chin, and whole assemblage of Features.

ASTROLOGY is a celestial science that treats of the doctrine of the stars, for the use and benefit of man, and it is proved, by daily observation and experience, that the fate of every person is not only written in the heavens at the time of their births, but also stamped and marked in the face and hands of every man. The one is called *Physiognomy;* the other *Chiromancy* or *Palmistry*—so that the fate of every person is written in three places, at the birth of every individual, viz.—first, in the heavens, secondly, in their faces, and thirdly, in their hands, all of which I shall explain in the course of this work. I shall now treat on the science of physiognomy. Observe the following rules:—

I.—The gentleman whose hair is very black and smooth, hanging far over his shoulders, and in large quantity, is mild but resolute; cool, until greatly provoked ; not much inclined to excess of any kind, but may be persuaded to it. He is constant in his attainments, and not liable to many misfortunes.

II.—A lady, of the same kind of hair, is moderate in all her desires, given to reflection, and though never violent in love, is steady in her attachments, and no enemy to its pleasures ; of a constitution neither vigorous nor feeble.

III.—If the hair is very black, short, and curling, the gentleman will be much given to liquor, rather quarrelsome, of an unsettled temper ; more amorous, and less steady in his undertakings, but ardent at the beginning of an enterprise. He will desire riches, but will often be disappointed in his wishes.

IV.—The same may be said of a lady.

V. — A gentleman with dark brown, long, and smooth hair, is generally of a robust constitution ; obstinate in his temper, eager in his pursuits, a lover of the fair sex, fond of variety, in his ordinary pursuits exceedingly curious, and of a flexible disposition. He will live long, unless guilty of early intemperance.

VI.—A lady of the same kind of hair will be nearly the same as the gentleman, but more steady in her conduct and attachments, especially in love. She will be of a good constitution, have many children, enjoy good health, and a reasonable share of happiness.

VII.—If the hair is short and bushy, it will make very little alteration in the gentleman or lady, but that the gentleman will be more forward to strike when provoked, and the lady will be more of a scold.

VIII.—A gentleman with light brown, long smooth hair, is of a peaceable, even, and rather generous temper; will prevent mischief if he can, but when very much provoked will strike furiously; but is afterwards sorry for his passion, and soon appeased; strongly attached to the company of ladies, and will protect them from insult. Upon the whole, he is an amicable character, affable and kind.

IX.—A lady of the same kind of hair is tender-hearted, but hasty in temper; neither obstinate nor haughty; her inclination to love never unreasonable; her constitution will be good, but she will be seldom very fortunate.

X.—A gentleman with fair hair will be of a weak constitution; given much to reflection, especially in religious matters; will be assiduous in his occupation, but not given to rambling; very moderate in his amorous wishes, but not live to old age.

XI.—A lady of this coloured hair is of a good constitution; not to be diverted from her purpose; passionate in love, never easy unless in company, and delights in flattery, especially for beauty; delights in dancing and strong exercises, and commonly lives to a great age.

XII.—A gentleman with long red hair is cunning, artful, and deceitful; very fond of traffic, restless in his disposition, constantly roving, and desirous of enjoying the pleasures of love. He is covetous after money, and spends it foolishly; he is indefatigable, and no obstacle will induce him to forsake his enterprize until he has seen the issue of it. He is rather timid but may pass for a man of courage.

XIII.—A lady of the same kind of hair is talka-

tive and vain ; her temper is impatient and fiery, not
submitting to contradiction ; she has a constant flow
of spirits, and much given to the pleasures of love.
However delicate her person may seem, her constitution is generally vigorous ; but she seldom lives to
old age ; her promises are seldom to be depended
upon, because the next object that engrosses her attention makes her forgetful of every thing that pre-
ceded it, and will always resent any disappointment
she may meet with.

I will now give some instructions concerning the
hair in other particulars :—

XIV.—If the hair falls off at the fore part of the
head, the person will be easily led, though otherwise
rational, and will often be duped, when he thinks he
is acting right ; he will also frequently meet with disappointments in money matters, which will either hurt
his credit, or force him to shorten his expenses.

XV.—If the hair falls off behind, he will be obstinate, peevish, passionate, and fond of commanding
others, and will grow angry if his advice is not followed.
He will be fond of hearing and telling old stories
about ghosts and fairies, but will be a good domestic man, and provide for his family to the utmost of
his power.

XVI.—If the hair forms an arch round the forehead, without being much indented at the temples,
both the gentleman and the lady will be innocent,
credulous, moderate in all their desires, and though
not ardent in their pursuits, will still be persevering.
They will be modest, good-natured, prosperous, and
happy.

XVII.—If the hair is indented at the temples, the

person will be affable, steady, good-natured, prudent, and attentive to business, of a solid constitution, and long lived.

XVIII.—If the hair descends low upon the forehead, the person will be selfish and designing; of a surly disposition, unsociable, given to drink and avarice, and his mind will always be intent upon the means of carrying on his schemes, &c.

XIX.—The forehead that is large, round and smooth, announces the lady or gentleman to be frank, open, generous, good-natured, and a safe companion; of a good understanding, and scorns a mean action; faithful to his promises, just in his dealings, steadfast to his engagements, sincere in his affections and will have good health.

XX.—If the forehead is flat in the middle, the gentleman or lady will be vainglorious, and little disposed to generosity; very tenacious of his honour, but brave; he will be fond of prying into the secrets of others, though not with an intention of betraying them; he will be fond of reading newspapers, history, novels, and plays; ardent, and very cautious of his own reputation, &c.

XXI.—If there is a hollow across the forehead, in the middle, with a ridge as of flesh above, and another below, the gentleman will be a good scholar, the lady a very great schemer, or attentive to whatever occupation she may be engaged in. They will be warm in argument or debate—they will be firm to any point they fix their minds upon, and by their perseverance will generally carry their object, yet they will meet with many crosses, but will bear them with patience.

XXII.—If the forehead jut out immediately at and over the eyebrows, running flat up to the hair, the gentleman or lady will be sullen, proud, insolent, imperious, and treacherous; they will be impatient when contradicted; apt to give great abuse, and to strike if they think they can do it with advantage. They will also impose upon any person, never forgive any injury, and make themselves many enemies.

XXIII.—If their temples are hollow, with the bones advancing towards the forehead on either side, so that the space between must be necessary flat, with a small channel or indenture rising from the upper part of the nose to the hair, the gentleman or lady will be of a daring and intrepid temper, introducing themselves into matters wherein they have no business, desirous of passing for wits, and of a subtle and enterprising nature; greedy of praise, quick in quarrel, and of a wandering disposition; very lewd, and full of resentment when they feel their pride hurt. They delight in mischief and riot.

XXIV.—If the eyebrows are very hairy, and that hair long and curled, with several of the hairs starting out, the gentleman or lady is of a gloomy disposition, litigious, and quarrelsome, although a coward; greedy after the affairs of this world, perpetually brooding over some melancholy subject, and not an agreeable companion. He will be diffident, penurious, and weak in his understanding; never addicted to any kind of learning. He will pretend much friendship, but will make his affected passion subservient to his pecuniary designs, and aiso given to drinking, &c.

XXV.—If a gentleman or lady has long eyebrows, with some long hairs, they will be of a fickle disposition, weak-minded, credulous, and vain, always seeking after novelties, and neglecting their own business; they will be talkative, pert, and disagreeable in company; very fond of contradiction, but will not bear disappointment patiently; and will also be much addicted to drinking, &c.

XXVI.—If the eyebrows are thick and even, that is, without any, or few starting hairs, the gentleman or lady will be of an agreeable temper, sound understanding, and tolerable wit; moderately addicted to pleasure, fearful of giving offence, but intrepid and persevering in support of right; charitable and generous, sincere in their professions of love and friendship, and enjoy a good constitution.

XXVII.—If the eyebrow is small, thin of hair, and even, the gentleman or lady will be weak - minded, timorous, superficial, and not to be depended on, they will be desirous of knowledge, but will not have patience and assiduity enough to give it the necessary attention; they will be desirous of praise for worthy actions, but will not have spirit or perseverance enough to perform them so as to attract the notice of wise men. They will be of a delicate constitution, &c.

XXVIII.—If the eyebrow is thick of hair towards the nose, and goes off suddenly very thin, ending in a point, the gentleman or lady will be surly, capricious, jealous, fretful, and easily provoked to rage; in their love they will be intemperate.

XXIX.—The eye that is large, full, prominent, and clear, denotes a gentleman or lady to be an of ingenious and candid disposition, void of deceit, and of an even, agreeable, and affable disposition; modest and bashful in love, though by no means an enemy to its gratification; firm, though not obstinate; of a good

understanding, of an agreeable but not brilliant wit;
but clear and just in argument, inclined to extravagance, and easily imposed upon.

XXX.—The eye that is small, but advanced in the
head, shows the gentleman or lady to be of a quick
wit, sound constitution, lively genius, very agreeable
company and conversation, good morals, but rather
inclined to jealousy; attentive to business, fond of
frequently changing his place, punctual in fulfilling
his engagements, warm in love, prosperous in his
undertakings, and fortunate in most things.

XXXI.—The gentleman or lady whose eyes are
sunk, is jealous, distrustful in their words and actions,
never to be depended upon; cunning in over-reach-
ing others, vain-glorious, and associates with lewd
company.

XXXII.—The gentleman or lady who squints, or
have their eyes turned awry, will be of a penurious
disposition, but punctual in their dealings.

XXXIII.—A black eye is lively, brisk, and penetrating, and proves the person who possesses it to be
of a sprightly wit, lively conversation, not easily
imposed upon, of a sound understanding, but if taken
on the weak side, may be led astray awhile.

XXXIV.—A hazel eye shows the person to be of
a subtle, piercing, and frolicsome turn, rather inclined
to be harsh, and sometimes mischievous, but good-
natured. He will be strongly inclined to love, and
not over delicate in the means of gratifying that
propensity.

XXXV.—A blue eye shows the person to be meek
and gentle, affable and good-natured, credulous, and
incapable of violent attachments; modest, cool, and

undisturbed by turbulent passions, of a strong memory, in constitution neither robust nor delicate, subject to no violent impression from the vicissitudes of life.

XXXVI.—A grey eye denotes the person to be of weak intellects, devoid of wit, but a plain plodding, downright drudge. He will be slow in learning anything that requires attention; he, however, will be just to the best of his understanding.

XXXVII.—A wall eye denotes the person to be hasty, passionate, and ungovernable, subject to sudden and violent anger; haughty to his equals and superiors, but mild and affable to his inferiors.

XXXVIII.—A red, or as it is vulgarly called, a saucer eye, denotes the person to be selfish, deceitful, and proud, furious in anger, fertile in the invention of plots, and indefatigable in his resolution to bring them to bear.

XXXIX.—A nose that comes even on the ridge, flat on the sides, with little or no hollow between the eyes, declares the man to be sulky, insolent, disdainful, treacherous, and self-sufficient; if it has a point descending over the nostrils, he is avaricious and unfeeling, vain-glorious and ignorant; peevish, jealous, quick in resentment, yet a coward at bottom.

XL.—A nose that rises with a sudden bulge a little below the eyes, and then falls into a kind of hollow below, is petulant and noisy, void of science, and of a light understanding.

XLI.—The nose that is small, slender, and peaked, shows the person to be of a fearful disposition, jealous, fretful, and insidious, ever suspicious of those

about him, catching at every word that he can inter-
pret to his own advantage to ground his dispute
upon, and also very curious to know what is said
and done.

XLII.—The nose that is small, tapering round in
the nostrils, and cocked up, shows the person to be
ingenious, smart, of a quick apprehension, giddy, and
seldom looking into consequences; but generous,
agreeable, so as to carefully avoid giving offence; but
resolute in doing himself justice when he receives an
injury.

XLIII.—The lips that are thick, soft, and long,
denote a person of weak intellects, credulous, and
slightly peevish; but by a little soothing easily
brought back to a good humour. He is immoderately addicted to the pleasures of love; yet he is
upright in his conduct, and of a timorous temper.

XLIV.—If the under lip is much thicker than the
upper, and more prominent, the person is weak in
intellect, but artful, knavish, and given to chicanery
to the full extent of his ability.

XLV.—The lips that are moderately plump and
even, declare the person to be good humoured,
humane, sensible, judicious, and just, neither giddy
nor torpid, but pursuing a just medium.

XLVI.—The lips that are thin, show the person to
be of a quick and lively imagination, ardent in the
pursuit of knowledge, indefatigable in labour, not too
much attached to money, eager in the pursuit of
love, more brave than otherwise, and happy in life.

XLVII.—The lips that are thin and sunk inwards,
denote the person to be of a subtle and persevering

disposition, and everlasting in hatred; in love or friendship more moderate and uncertain.

XLVIII.—A round chin, with a hollow between it and the lip, shows the person to be good-humoured, kind, and honest; sincere in friendship, and ardent in love; his understanding is good, and his genius capacious. If he has a dimple, better still.

XLIX.—The chin that comes down flat from the edge of the lip, and ends in a kind of chisel form, shows the person to be silly, credulous, ill-tempered, and greedy of unmerited honours; captious, wavering and unsteady; affects great modesty, but will not scruple to do the vilest actions, when he thinks himself secure from discovery.

L.—The chin pointed upwards, shows the person to be given to contrivances. However fair he may speak to you, you can never depend on his friendship, as his purpose is to make you subservient to his own designs. In love his generosity will be of the same stamp.

LI.—Of the face in general: the person whose features are strong, coarse, and unpleasant to the eye, is of a selfish, brutal, rough, and unsociable disposition; greedy of money, harsh in expressions, but will sometimes fawn with a bad grace to gain his own selfish ends.

LII.—The face that is plump, round, and ruddy, denotes the person to be of an agreeable temper, a safe companion, hearty, and jovial, fond of company, of sound principles and a clear understanding, faithful in love, &c.

LIII.—The face that is thin, smooth, and even, with well proportioned features, shows the person to be of a good disposition, but penetrating and active; somewhat inclined to suspicion, yet of an agreeable conversation ; assiduous in the pursuits of knowledge, and strongly addicted to the delights of love.

LIV.—A face whose cheek bones jut out with thin jaws, is of a restless and thinking disposition; fretful, &c.

LV.—A face that is pale by nature, denotes a timorous disposition, but greatly desirous of carnal pleasures.

LVI.—A face that is unequally red, whether streaked, or appearing in spots, shows the person to be weak both in mind and body, yielding easily to affliction and sickness.

LVII.—A face blotched, shows the person to be addicted to drinking and vice, and not even free from any vice, though they have frequently the art to conceal the inclination.

LVIII.—The head that is large and round, shows that the person has a tolerable understanding, but not near so good as he imagines; however, upon the whole, he is rather harmless, and not so much given to vice.

LIX.—The head that is small and round, or if the face comes tapering, shows the person of an acute, penetrating disposition, much given to bantering and humour, but of very great sensibility, &c.

LX.—The head that is flat on either side, and deep from the face to the back, shows the person to be of a good understanding, deep penetration, great memory, and of an even and agreeable temper, but slow of belief, and not easily imposed upon.

———

OF CHIROMANCY, OR PALMISTRY.

MENSA.

THE practical part of Chiromancy, is that which gathereth probable predictions from lines, the places of the planets in the hand, and from the notes and characters every where posited and marked out in the hands and fingers. Wherefore let the following series be duly observed :—

1.—*Cardiaca,* or the line of life.
2.—*Epatica,* or the liver line; also called the natural mean.

3.—*Cephalica,* or the line of the head and brain.
4.—*Thoralis,* or the table line.

5.—*Restricta*, or the dragon's tail.

6.—*Via Solis*, or the sun's way.

7.—*Via Luctea*, or milky way.

8.—*Via Saturnia*, or Saturn's way.

9.—*Cingulum Veneris*, or the girdle of Venus.

10.—*Via Martis*, or the way of Mars.

11.—*Mons Veneris*, or the mound of Venus.

12.—*Cavea Martis*, or the Cave of Mars.

13.—*Mons Jovis*, or Jupiter's mount.

14.—*Mons Saturn*, or Saturn's mount.

15.—*Mons Solis*, or the Sun's mount.

16.—*Locus Lunœ*, or the Moon's place.

17.—*Mons Mercurii*, or the Mount of Mercury.

18.—*Mensa*, or the table containing the part of fortune.

19.—*Pollex*, or the thumb.

20.—*Indax*, or the fore finger.

21.—*Medius*, or the middle finger.

22.—*Annularis*, or the ring finger.

23.—*Auricularis*, or the little finger.

QUESTION.

Whether we must give judgment by the right hand or left.

It is certain, that in one hand the lines and other signatures are very often more manifest, and more plainly to be seen than in the other, as well in the hands of gentlemen as ladies. Wherefore, a question arises, whether in both sexes the right or left hand is to be taken, or whether the right hand of a gentleman and the left of a lady only.

ANSWER.

That hand which exhibits the lines thereof most

clearly, and abounds with a series of characters and signs, yet so, as that the other, whose lines are more obscure, may pay its contribution. If in both hands they consent and appear to be fair and comely, they declare constancy of fortune and health. The cause of which diversity is this : he who is born in the day time, and hath a masculine planet (the Sun, Saturn, Jupiter, or Mars) lord of his geniture, bears the more remarkable signs in his right hand, especially when the sign ascending is also masculine. The contrary happens to them that are born by night, as often as a feminine planet predominates. If both hands agree, it must be that in a diurnal nativity the feminine planets rule ; or that there is a mixture of masculine and feminine ; so in the night by the contrary reason, which diversity must necessarily be observed.

I.—OF THE LINE OF LIFE.

This is called Cardiaca, or the Heart Line.

1.—This being broad, of a lively colour, and decently drawn in its bounds, without intersections and points, shows the party long lived, and subject but to few diseases.

2.—If slender, short, and dissected with obverse little lines, and deformed either by a pale or black colour, it presages weakness of the body, sickness and a short life.

3.—If orderly joined to the natural mean, and beautified in the angle with parallels, or a little across, it argues a good wit, or an evenness of nature.

4.—If the same have branches in the upper parts thereof, extending themselves towards the natural mean, it signifies riches and honour.

5.—If these branches be extended towards the restricta, it threatens poverty, deceits, and unfaithfulness of servants.

6.—If in this line there be found some confused lines, like hairs, be assured of diseases, and they to happen in the first age. When they appear below, if towards the cavea, in the middle ; if towards the patica, in declining age.

7.—If this line be anywhere broken, it threatens extreme danger of life in that part of the age which the place of the breach showeth. For you may find out the dangerous or deceased years of your age ; this line being divided into seventy parts, you must begin your number and account from the lower part thereof, near the restricta, for the number falling where the branch is, determines the year.

8.—If the character of the sun (as commonly it is made by astrologers) be ever found in this line, it presages the loss of an eye.   But, if two such characters, the loss of both eyes.

9.—A line ascending from the vital, under its congress and the epactica to the tuberculum of Saturn, showeth an envious man, who rejoiceth at another's calamity, the scite of others concurring.—This also shows a perilous Saturnine disease in that wherein it touches the vital, and it is worse if it cut the same.

10.—But such a line passing from the vital to the annular, or ring finger, promiseth honours to ensue, from or by the means of some famous lady, to receive some great favour or present from a lady of honour.

11.—The vital line being thicker than ordinary at

the end under the fore finger, denotes a laborious old age.

12.—A line passing through the vital to the cavea of Mars, foretells of wounds and fevers, and also of misfortunes in journeys.

II.—OF THE EPATICA, OR NATURAL MEAN.

1.—This line being straight, continued, and not dissected by obverse little lines, denotes a healthful body.

2.—If short or broken, and reach not beyond the concave of the hand, it shows disease and short life.

3.—By how much more the same is produced, by so much longer the life may be warranted.

4.—If cut at the end thereof by a small intervening line, it threatens poverty in old age.

5.—If in the upper part it be distant from the vital by a great space, it shows distemperatures of the heart, as palpitations, syncope, &c.

6.—This also shows prodigality, especially if the table be broad.

7.—If tortuous (turning several ways,) unequal, of a different colour, and dissected, it argues an evil state of the liver. Covetousness also, and a depravity of nature and wit, especially if it be under the region of the middle finger, and near the cardiaca, thereby making a short or narrow triangle.

8.—If decently drawn and well coloured, it is a sign of a cheerful and ingenuous disposition.

9.—If it has a sister, it promises inheritances.

10.—If continued with little hard knots, it denotes manslaughters, perpetrated or committed, according to the number of knots.

11.—If therein is a cross under the region of the middle finger, it shows speedy death.

12.—If it terminates with a fork towards the ferient, it is a sign of depraved wit, hypocrisy, and evil manners.

13.—When it tend to the mensa, it is a token of a slanderous tongue, and of envy.

14.—When it projects a cleft through the vital to the mons veneris, and the sister of Mars, especially if the same be of a ruddy colour, it warns to be aware of thieves, and intimates fraud and deceit of enemies.

15.—This cleft likewise insinuates a most vehement heat of the liver, proceeding from the rays of Mars; so that the life becomes in danger, seeing that the line of life is dissected.

16.—This line having a breach, yet such a one continued shows that the manner of life will be, or is already changed; and in a declining age if the breach be under the ring finger. If under the middle finger, in the strength of years.

III.—OF THE CEPHALICA.

1.—This is called the line of the head and brain, which, if it connects the lines of the liver and heart in a triangular form, have a lively colour, and no intersection falling out between, declares a man of prudence, and of good wit and fortune.

2.—By how much more decent the triangle is, so much better shall the temperature, wit, and courage be. But if it be obtuse, it argues an evil disposed nature, and a man that is rude. If no triangle, far worse.

3.—The superior being a right angle, or not very

acute foretells the best temperature of heart ; but when it is too acute, especially if it touch the line of life, upon the region of the middle finger it argues covetousness.

4.—The left angle, if it be made upon the natural mean in the ferient, and be a right angle, confirms the goodness of intellect.

5.—When the cephalica projects unequal clefts to the mons lunæ, making unusual characters ; in the gentleman it denotes weakness of brain, and dangerous sea voyages. But in the ladies' hands it shows frequent sorrows of mind, and difficulties in child-bearing.

6.—Equal lines (thus projected) presage the contrary in both sexes, viz : in gentlemen, a good composure of the brain, and fortunate voyages by sea. In ladies, cheerfulness and felicity in child-bearing.

7.—One thing is peculiar to the cephalica ; if it project a cleft, or a manifest star, upwards to the cavea martis, it signifies boldness, &c. If it let fall the same downwards, thefts, &c.

8.—The cephalica, jointed to the dragon's tail, by a remarkable concourse, promises a prudent and joyful age.

9.—The same drawn upwards in the shape of a fork, towards the part of fortune, signifies subtlety in managing affairs, and also craftiness either to good or bad.

10.—If in this said fork a mark appears resembling the part of fortune, as it is noted by astrologers, that gives an assurance of riches and honour to succeed by ingenuity and art.

IV.—OF THE THORAL LINE.

1.—This is called the line of fortune, and also the mensa, because it makes up the table of the hand. When it is long enough, and without incisures, it argues due strength in the principal members of man, and constancy; the contrary if it be short, crooked, cut or parted.

2.—If it terminate under the mount of Saturn, it shows a vain fellow.

3.—If projecting small branches to the mount of Jupiter, it promises honours.

4.—If there it be naked and simple, it is a sign of poverty and want.

5.—If cutting the mouth of Jupiter; crulty of mind and disposition, with excessive wrath.

6.—If it projects a branch between the fore and middle finger in a gentleman, it threateneth a wound in his head; in a lady, danger in child-bearing.

7.—Three lines ascending from this line, viz., one to the space between the middle and fore finger, a second to the space between the middle and ring finger, and a third to the space between the ring and the little finger, argues a contentious person in many respects.

8.—A little line only thus drawn to the interval or space between the middle finger and the ring finger, sorrow, or labour.

9.—If annexed to the natural mean, so that it makes an acute angle, sorrow and labour.

10.—If the natural mean be wanting, and the thoral annexed to the vital, it threatens decollation, or a deadly wound.

11.—If no mensa at all, it shows a man malevolent, contentious, faithless and inconstant.

12.—Confused little lines in the mensa, denote sickness; if under Mercury, in the former part of the age; under the sun, in the prime thereof; under the middle finger, in old age.

13.—When in this line there are certain points observed, they argue strength of the genitals, and burning lust.

V.—OF THE CAUDA DRACONIS, OR THE RESTRICTA, AND THE LINES ARISING THENCE.

1 .—If this be double or treble, and drawn by a right and continued track, it promiseth a good composure of the body.

2.—That line nearest the hand continued, and of a good colour, assureth of great riches.

3.—But if the same line be cut in the middle, crooked, and very pale, it announces a debility of body and want of all things.

4.—A cross or star upon the restricta, foreshows tranquillity of life in old age.

5.—If there be a star, simple or double, or any lines near the tuberculum of the thumb, in ladies they denote misfortune or infamy.

6.—A line running from the restricta through the mons veneris, presageth adversities, either by the means of some kindred or a wife.

7.—A line extended from the restricta to the mons lunæ denotes adversities and private enemies; if it be crooked, it doubles the evil, and betokeneth perpetual servitude.

8.—Such a line also being clear and straight, and

reaching so far as the region of the moon, foretells many journeys by sea and land.

9.—If it extend to the tuberculum of the fore finger, it informs the gentleman that he shall live in a foreign country in great estimation.

10.—If to the epatica, it argues an honest behaviour, and prolongeth life.

11.—If to the mons solis (be it simple or double), it shows exceeding good, and enableth to govern or rule in great affairs.

12.—By the same reason, if it pass to the mons Mercurii, it betokeneth the gentleman is of a sufficient capacity for any employment. But if it reach not the mons Mercurii, but is broken about the middle and end beneath the mons Mercurii, that denotes a prating fellow, &c.

13.—If directly ascending to the mons Saturni, it signifies a good position of Saturn in the geniture, whose decree will shortly follow. But, if crookedly towards the restricta and the epatica specially, it shows man laborious, &c.

VI.—OF THE VIA SOLIS, OR THE SUN'S WAY.

This being whole, equally drawn, and well coloured, promiseth the favour of great men and great honour. But if dissected and unequal, the contrary, and exposes to divers impediments, and envy in attaining the same.

VII.—OF THE VIA LACTEA, OR MILKY WAY.

This, well proportioned and continued, presages that journeys will be fortunate by sea and land, as ready wit, and the favour of the ladies (Venus assenting), of a composed and graceful speech; but, if distorted, it argues infelicity and lies; but whole and ascending to the little finger, it is a happy sign.

VIII.—OF THE SATURNIA, OR LINE OF SATURN.

1.—This being fully protracted to the middle finger, shows both profound cogitations, and fortunate events in counsels and actions.

2.—Combust or deficient, portends many misfortunes, unless other positions favour it.

3.—Bending backwards in the cavea of the hand, towards the ferient, in the form of a semi-circle, threatens imprisonment.

4.—A line drawn from the vital through the epatica to the tuberculum of Saturn (if it touch the Saturnia), the same.

IX.—OF THE CINGULUM VENERIS, OR THE GIRDLE OF VENUS.

If this line have a sister, it argues intemperance and lust in both sexes, and baseness in venereal congression, a filthy man, who abhors not an unnatural crime; and, if dissected and troubled, losses and infamy by reason of lusts.

X.—OF THE VIA MARTIS, THE WAY OR LINE OF MARS, OR THE VITAL SISTER.

This line (as often as it appeareth) augments and strengthens the things signified by the cardiaca, but particularly, it promises good success in war, provided it be clear and red.

Some observations concerning Lines.

1.—The quantity of all lines must be wisely observed, that is, the length and depth; also their quality, that is, their complexion and shape, whether they are crooked or straight, next their action, which is to touch or cut other lines. Their passion to be touched or cut off others; and lastly, their place and position.

2.—We must know that the lines are sometimes prolonged until certain years of our age, otherwise shortened; now they wax pale, then become plain and strong, and luxuriate with a kind of redness, and this in the principal as less principal lines. Again, as touching the less principal, and such as are found in the tubercula of the planets, it is most certain, that some do one time vanish, and at another time others rise of a different shape and complexion: the cause of which, is the various progressions of the alphabetical places in their nativities: that is fortunate and unfortunate, to the influence of which man himself is very subject. The signs of his hand are presented different times with quite different faces. *Such a virtue, such a love resideth in the imagination of the greater world towards the lesser.* And, therefore, the most studious in chiromancy cannot attain the knowledge of particulars by one inspection only, made to a certain year of the person's age.

OF THE PLANETS.

The planets also administer in judgment from their respective place, for if they are happy and benevolent, good things are portended, but being unhappy and froward, judge the contrary. Those planets are termed benevolent, in whose tubercula and places the accustomed lines are found to be equal, their characters fair and proportionable, as a cross, stars, three or four parallel lines, ladders, little branches, a quadrangular, the character of Jupiter. But the froward and unfortunate are those planets whose tubercula and places are deformed with troubled lines and uncouth figures; as a lame and interrupted semi-circle, gridirons, the character of Saturn.

XI.—VENUS.

Venus shining well in her tuberculum presents a clear star, or furrows that are red and transversely parallel, and so often as her tuberculum is much elevated, makes such men to be merry, cheerful, luxurious; yet amorous, comely, and libidinous, very honest and just, with whom friendship is permanent.

She renders the body somewhat tall, the eyes beautiful, sparkling, alluring, and tempting, the hair thick and curling; she instils a spotless and noble mind, yet often makes men full of boasting and inconsistency. She inclines the mind to music, &c.; according to the strength of the geniture, she denotes priests, apothecaries, &c.

Being unfortunate she causeth lasciviousness, incontinency, and if you find a cross also, near the first joint of the thumb, it denotes an adulterer. If the place of Venus be untilled, it points out an effeminate and sorrowful person, addicted to jesting.

XII.—MARS.

Mars, so often as his sister appeareth red, clear, and well drawn, and when star or cross is found in his cavea, denotes such as are bold, stout, warlike, contentious, strong, and lusty; imperious; the hair for the most part yellow, the eyes from black waxing red and terrible. If Jupiter participate, he possesses the gall, the reins, the back, the liver, &c.

XIII.—JUPITER.

Jupiter is fortunate when in his region he exhibits signs auspicious, that is, if there be a star or a double cross, parallel lines, or a line well drawn from the vital to his tuberculum, he signifies men noble, honest, benevolent, merry, just, beautiful, formidable, and happy, such as have comely eyes, thick hairs, and a grave gesture. These men are preferred to great dignities, and esteem their wives, sons, honest and good men. In men, Jupiter rules the liver, blood, ribs, lungs, and gristles. But, if unfortunate, he often throws a man into peril ; if there be half a gridiron in his tuberculum, it betokeneth losses ; otherwise thus constituted, he causeth grief, cramps, inflammations of the lungs, and flatulence ; if a line transversely cut his tuberculum, and tend to the place of Saturn, making those little hairs, it threatens apoplexy. But, if you find a cross, or a clear red star in his tuberculum, he gives honours, riches, and public rewards.

XIV.—SATURN.

Saturn is happily placed, when his line runs to his region, but less happy when he presents some inauspicious characters ; if he shows confused and unfortunate signs, he governs the spleen, bones, and bladder. When fortunate, he makes men silent, provident, wise in counsels, sorrowful, studious, and ambitious. And these are slender of body, somewhat tall, pale, feeble, hair blackish, eyes hollow ; they are fortunate in tilling ground, and in metals of all sorts, yet careless of their wives, and less addicted to the pleasures of love. If Saturn be unfortunate, he makes men sorrowful, sordid, humble, liars, malicious, envious,

&c. and full of griefs and anxieties. A gross line running from the interval of the middle and fore finger to the mensa, and breaking or interrupting it, denotes diseases or wounds in the lower part of the body.

XV.—SOL.

If the sun do fortunately rule, he makes men faithful, ingenious, honoured, high-minded, wise, humane, religious, just, moderate, aged. He gives a body well composed, and adorns it with yellow hair. He governs the heart, midriff, nerves, &c. But, if unfortunate, he gives men proud, boasters, and immodest. He brings fluxes of rheums upon the eyes, trembling of the heart, syncope, &c,

XVI.—LUNA.

The moon, happy and fortunate, makes men famous, honest, and honourable, and of a large body, yet well-proportioned; but, if dissenting in the other, inconstant in life and action. She rules the brain, stomach, and belly. If unfortunate, she portends an inconstant kind of life, weakness, and anxieties; she thus causeth the paralysis, &c. A commotion of the members, an epilepsy, canker, spots in the body, severe cholic, and more especially when the lines in the tuberculum of the moon appear very pale; if there be fair signatures near the ferient they denote happiness in journeys and messages. To the woman, felicity and fertility in child-bearing, ominous signs the contrary.

XVII.—MERCURY.

Mercury, happy and fortunate, makes men ingenious, desirous of science, and seeking diligently after secrets; orators, poets, philosophers, astrologicians, fortune-tellers, mathematicians, and merchants. He governs the tongue and memory.

XVIII.—The Mensa, or Part of Fortune.

1.—This space being great and broad, and the figure decent, declares a liberal man, magnanimous, and of a long life.

2.—But if small and narrow, it indicates a slender fortune and fearfulness.

3.—A cross or star within it, clear and well proportioned, especially under the region of the ring finger, betokeneth honours and dignities to ensue from great and noble personages. If the character of Jupiter, it promises great ecclesiastical dignities.

4.—The same star or cross tripled, portends good fortune but if cut by confused little lines, it denotes anxieties and labours in defending his honours, if they are under the region of the ring finger.

5.—A cross or star in the uppermost part of the mensa, is a sign of fortunate journeys.

6.—The mensa sharpened by the concourse of the thoral and cardiac lines, point out deceits and danger of life.

7.—If no mensa be found in the hand, it shows obscurity both of life and fortune.

8.—Good and equal lines in this space declare the fortune to be good, but if evil and discomposed, they quite overthrow it.

9.—A little circle shows great wit, and the obtaining of science.

XIX.—The Pollex, or Thumb.

Overthwart lines, clear and long under the nail and joint of the thumb, confer riches and honour.

A line passing from the upper joint of the thumb to the cardiaca, threatens a violent death, or danger, by some married lady. Lines much dispersed in the lower joint of the thumb, describe men contentious and given to scolding. A line surrounding the thumb, in the middle joint, portends the man will be hanged. Equal furrows under the lower joint, argue riches and possessions. If the first or second joints want incisures, it shows idleness.

XX.—THE INDEX, OR FORE FINGER.

Many lines in the uppermost joint, proceeding overthwartly, denote inheritances; if so in the middle joint, an envious and evil disposed person.

Right lines between these joints, declare a numerous issue. In gentlemen, bitterness of the tongue. If in the first joint near Jupiter's mouth, they manifest a jovial disposition. That woman who hath a star in the same place, will be unchaste.

XXI.—MEDIUS, OR THE MIDDLE FINGER.

This finger presenting little gridirons in the joints declares melancholy wit, but if equal lines, fortune by metals, &c. A star presages death by drowning, &c. If a gross line be extended from its root through the whole finger to the end of the last joint, it argues folly and madness.

XXII.—ANNULARIS, OR THE KING FINGER.

A line rising from mons solis, and ascending by a right track through its joints, shows a noble frame. Equal lines in the first joint, honours and riches. Overthwart lines, the enmity of great men. If these lines are intersected, it is better.

XXIII.—AURICULARIS, OR LITLLE FINGER.

From the joint thereof, as from the mount itself, are judgments passed concerning merchandise, favours: a star in the first joint near the tuberculum, argues ingenuity and eloquence. Other obtuse signs the contrary ; unfortunate signs in the first and second joints, mark a thief and deceitful person. If adverse lines in the last joint, inconstancy. Some truly predict the number of wives from the little lines in the mons Mercurii at the outmost part of the hand. If the end of this finger touch not the last joint of the ring finger, it signifies a wife imperious, as is often proved.

MOUNTS AND FINGERS.

The mounts being adorned with good figures and characters, indicates a good issue ; being vitiated with confused lines, they also threaten the contrary as well on the fingers as mounts, except restrained by the confederacy of other fortunate lines.

2.—There are likewise the twelve signs of the Zodiac on the fingers. The signification of the lines from the mouths of the planets up to the fingers show their effect chiefly when the sun, or principal significator, as lord of the ascendant, is in those signs, ruling the parts where they terminate, as a line passing from the mount of Saturn to the first point of the middle finger would give improvement, when the Sun was in Pisces. If to the second, in Aquarius. The first joint near the mount of the finger must be attributed to the first part of the age, the second to the prime of life ; to last to old age.

3.—Lastly. The structure of the hand itself is admirable in respect to the proportion it bears to the face, and certain parts thereof, as :—

1.—The whole hand is of equal length with the face.

2.—The greater joint of the fore finger equals the height of the forehead.

3.—The other two is the length of the nose, viz., from the intercella, or place between the eyebrows, to the tip of the nostrils.

4.—The first and greater joint of the middle finger, is just as long as it is between the bottom of the chin and the top of the under lip.

5.—The third joint of the same finger is as long as the distance between the mouth and the lower part of the nostrils.

6.—The largest joint of the thumb, the width of the mouth.

7.—The distance between the bottom of the chin, and the top of the lower lip the same.

8.—The lesser joint of the thumb is equal to the distance between the top of the under lip, and the lower part of the nostrils. The nails are the half of their respective uppermost joints which they call omychios.

PRACTICE OF CHIROMANCY.—See Engraving.

Five planets are well placed in their own prerogatives, Saturn and Mercury in reception by houses, and located in their own triplicity; so Jupiter and Mars assume a just power by their reception of houses. Venus in her exaltation, in the angle of the earth; lastly, the moon in a sign of her own nature, in conjunction with Venus and caput draconis. The moon having not as yet obtained her due light from the sun, is placed here very silent; Saturn and Mercury are united by a trine, the part of fortune rising so near the Scorpion's heart, of the nature of Mars and Jupiter; Venus and Jupiter are prime rulers of this nativity, Saturn and Mercury participating.

1.—A long life is promised from the horoscope and the luminaries being not impedite, although the moon is now afflicted by a quartile of Mars. Yet the progress of the horoscope is first to the opposition of Saturn, whereof

2.—His temperature excels by an equal mixture of humours, for he receiveth his ferment from the profusion of Jupiter and Venus; Saturn and Mercury giving a melancholy cast.

3.—Hence Jupiter makes such as are born under him, just, and wise, and addicted to peaceable counsels; such also are desirous of renown.

4.—Venus, therefore, and Jupiter, promise great felicity in civil and ecclesiastical affairs.

5.—Here are testimonies of an excellent ingenuity, (1) Mercury in Aquarius suscitates the strength thereof; (2) there is also a reception from houses, and a partile trine between him and Saturn; (3) Venus angular doth the like; (4) especially as the moon and the dragon's head are together in the same angle; (5) Mercury and the moon are asyntheti, pure and not vitiated, yet both behold the horoscope; the moon by a platic trine, and Mercury by a partile quartile.

6.—Jupiter, lord of the second direct in motion, and received by Mars, assures abundance of wealth. The part of fortune augments this signification, being posited so near the second, where he is disposed of, and aspected by Jupiter. These riches take their increase from services faithfully performed, and more abundantly in the third or latter part of his age.

7.—Mercury, lord of the tenth house, and having convenient society with Saturn, presages dignities. Jupiter and Venus equally share the rule in this nativity, and they reward the native with dignities.

8.—Your neighbours or kindred shall occasion you damage in household goods or affairs, and you shall expend much money in building.

9.—Mars, lord of the sixth house, engendereth hot diseases, yet they are not so violent because of Jupiter's interposition; also Mars, in Sagittarius causes pain in the joints of the feet. If found in that sign, and in the sixth, he brings the gout, not to be taken away but by the influence of Sagittarius, Pisces, deducted from heaven itself.

10.—Your death will be natural by the means of chronical infirmity proceeding principally from Saturn, such as distillations upon the breast, lungs, spleen, &c. Old age is a disease, and an easy passage to death.

11.—The sun and moon, disposing of the ninth house, show honourable journeys. Mercury, well posited in the third, causeth journeys, honours, and dignities.

12.—Venus, lady of the eleventh house, concerns a multitude of the best friends. Yet Mars beholding Venus by a quartile, will stir up the envy of persons, sowing dissensions, and inverting goodness.

13.—Venus gives victory over enemies, whereof there are but few denounced, for she is lady of the seventh angular, and in her exaltation.

14.—Your marriage will be fortunate in respect to riches, yet beware of the faithless brawling, and luxurious quadrature of Mars.

The Signs of the Four Angels.

15.—Scorpio ascending, gives the native elegant wit, plenty of discourse; it instilleth great vices, as infidelity, envy, covetousness, deceit, ingratitude, which come by our depraved nature, but which learning, religion, and reason ought to exterminate.

16.—Virgo culminating, generally raises the native to magistracy. It confers great authority and benefits to others.

17.—Taurus in the west angle, presents you with such as you will see oppressed by sundry kinds of misfortunes; this sign incites you to love, luxury, feasting, pleasures, and jesting.

18.—Pisces posited in the fourth, endues the mind with much faith, integrity, and dexterity of wit, whereby they gain great authority; they delight to walk and dwell near rivers.

The Planets in the Houses of Heaven.

19.—The sun in the third, presages journeys, in the cause of honour. He brings a mutation of places and honour in foreign countries.

20.—Mercury, where well posited renders a man most learned in science and ingenious inventions, fortunate ecclesiastically, in writing, merchandise.

21.—Venus well collected in the fourth, will give large possessions and habitations, chiefly in the latter part of your age, which she declares honourable.

22.—Mars in the first, and not unfortunate, makes a man courageous, rash, bold; sometimes presaging wounds in the head and face.

23.—Jupiter in the fifth gives fortunate and obedient children, and rewards from great men. He makes fortunate in embassies.

24.—Saturn thus located in the eighth, gives many inheritances by legacies. He there threatens death by catarrhs, coughs, consumptions, and sometimes the pestilence.

THE PLANETS IN THE SIGNS OF THE ZODIAC.

25.—The sun in the house of Saturn, makes the vital virtue more robust and compact, and a longer life than ordinary.

26.—The moon in the house of Jupiter, promotes all things that are good; yet being here afflicted by the quartile of Mars, excites some strife in possessions, and often small fevers.

27.—Saturn in the house of Mercury, gives profound wit, and occult sciences.

28.—Jupiter in the house of Mars, indifferently well affected, makes a man victorious.

29.—Mars in the mansion of Jupiter, renders the native very gracious with princes and noblemen, and under them to have authority.

30.—Venus in the house of Jupiter, bestows many benefits, either by the means of ladies, or of ecclesiastical preferments. She also makes discreet, honest, faithful, and healthful; sometimes will cause strife, because Venus is exposed to the quadrature of Mars.

31.—Mercury in the house of Saturn, always gives a profound wit, and a person that is ever anxious to obtain all sciences.

THE LORDS OF THE HOUSES.

32.—The lord of the horoscope being received by

Jupiter, and being in reception also by houses, declares a generous mind.

33.—The lord of the second in the fifth, increases wealth by means of receiving rewards and premiums bestowed by great men.

34.—The lord of the third in the eighth, causes journeys either on behalf of some that are dead, or concerning legacies. He often destroys elder brothers, &c., or is often employed on sudden business.

35.—The lord of the fourth in the fifth, gives success in tilling the ground, and in navigation.

36.—The lord of the fifth in the ascendant, causes gladness from things immovable, as the building of good houses, fortunate in gaming, and comfort with children, who will make good and bold martial men.

37.—Mars, lord of the sixth of the first, causes many hot diseases; but this is moderated by the reception and position of Jupiter.

38.—The lady of the seventh in the fourth, presageth strife about the father's or wife's inheritance, because she is afflicted by Mars.

39.—The lord of the eighth in the third, shows that the native shall survive all his brothers, but he shows death in a foreign country.

40.—The lord of the ninth in the third, causeth many journeys for dignities, &c.

41.—The lord of the tenth in the third, makes the native more honourable than his brethren.

42.—The lady of the eleventh in the fourth, denotes a second fortune, especially in old age, and that by means of her father.

43.—The lady of the twelfth in the fourth, shows contention for possession of property.

Judgment by the Hand enclosed in the Figure.

1.—The vital is continued, but marked with some slender incisures; you will be afflicted with diseases about your 14th, 30th, and 40th year.

2.—Venus is fortunate in this nativity, and hath raised her region with the accustomed furrows.

3.—The epatica decently drawn, and without sections, argues a good temperature of the liver, health of body, and a life that is long enough.

4.—The mensa full of branches denotes riches.

5.—The mensa formed by a decent space, promiscuously bearing the characters of Jupiter under the region of the annular is an argument of honours, chiefly ecclesiastical. Observe, that the sun and the moon claim the dominion of the ninth house in this nativity.

6.—The place of Jupiter beautified with a most clear little line, the same; so likewise the tuberculum of the sun decently furrowed.

7.—The moon's region presenting a clear incisure, denotes journeys.

8.—The dominion of Mercury is almost obvious, in that he excellently adorneth his region, as also the first joint of the auricular.

9.—The cephalica contributes to the wit, in that it decently composeth the triangle. Jupiter, Venus, and Mercury, do the like.

10.—Saturn portends a disease, in that he bears a character under his finger.

11.—The parallel lines which run through the midst of the hand towards the ferient, confirm the arguments of felicity.

12.—The Saturnia produced to the epatica, shows an upright heart, judgment, and manners. With a cross about the restricta, argues a peaceable and honourable old age.

Observe.—In the use of purgative medicines, you must observe the moon being in Scorpio, Aquarius, and the third decade of Pisces, though she be not joined to Jupiter or Venus; for the conjunction of these planets with the moon, inhibits the virtue of the purgative medicine as they affect the body, and incline the medicine to the nature of nourishment. In buying houses, in journeys, and administrations, &c., let the moon be in Aries, Taurus, Cancer, Libra, or Aquarius, and aspected by one or both of the fortunate planets; and let the day of the week be Wednesday, Thursday, or Friday.

GEOMANCY.

1.—Rubius being posited in the ascendant, shows a deceitful, wicked person, much given to vice of every kind. These vices, so predominant in us, must be destroyed by the power of God.

2.—Acquisitio in the second, brings great riches to the native.

3.—Tristitia and Cancer in the third, shows the death of your brethren, and danger from thieves.

4.—Letitia in the fourth, indicates land and inheritances, with some trouble and contention attending the same.

5.—Puer in the fifth, valiant children, &c.

6.—Amissio in the sixth, shows hot diseases.

7.—Amissio and Albus in the seventh, gives you a talkative and scolding wife.

8.—Populus in the eigth, promises good legacies, and a long life, natural death, and perhaps after some long voyage.

9.—Fortuna Major in the ninth, gives ecclesiastical preferments, and the favour of great men.

10.—Conjunctio in the tenth, gives great honour, by means of your learning and abilities.

11.—Puella in the eleventh, gives you many friends, even ladies of high rank.

12.—Rubius in the twelfth, will give you private enemies, who will cause trouble.

OF MOLES.

Showing their Situation, and their Indication of a Person's Disposition, and future Lot in Life.

Though moles are nothing else than excrescences, which proceed from the state of the blood whilst the fœtus is confined in the womb, yet they are not given in vain, as they are generally characteristic of the disposition and temper. It is proved by daily experience that from the shape, situation, and other circumstances, they bear a strong analogy to the events which are to happen to a person in future life.

MARKS, SCARS, OR MOLES.

From the Figure of the Heavens at the time of Birth, without any other reference whatsoever.

IN the first place, observe what sign is upon the cusp of the ascendant, and in that part of the native's body which that sign governs, there will be a mole. For instance, if Aries be the sign ascending at the

time of birth, the mole will be on the head or face;
if Taurus, on the neck or throat; if Gemini, on the
arms or shoulders; if Cancer, on the breast; and on
any other part which the sign ascending shall govern.
Observe next, in which of the houses the lord of the
ascendant is posited, and in that part of the body the
sign governs which falls upon the cusp of that house,
the native will have another mole. Observe the sign
descending on the cusp of the sixth house, and in
whatever part of the body that sign governs, the native will find another mole; and upon that member
also which is signified by the sign, wherein the lord
of the sixth house is posited, will be found another.

Observe what sign the moon is posited in, and in
that part of the body which is governed by it, shall
the native or querent find another mole. If the
planet Saturn be the significator, the mole is of a dark
colour. If Mars be the significator, and in a fiery
sign, it resembles a scar, cut, or dent in the flesh, but
in any other sign it is a red mole. If Jupiter be the
significator, the mole is of a bluish cast. If the sun,
of an olive or chestnut colour. If Venus, yellow; if
Mercury, of a pale lead colour; if the moon, whitish,
or of the colour of that planet with which she is in
aspect. And if the planet which gives the mole be
much impedited or afflicted, the mark or mole will
be larger or more visible to the eye.

If the sign and planet which give the mark or mole
be masculine, it is situated on the right side of the
body; but if feminine, on the left side. If the significator or planet which gives the mole, be from the
cusp of the ascendant to the cusp of the seventh in
the twelfth, eleventh, tenth, ninth, eighth, or seventh
house, the mark or mole will be on the fore part of
the body; but if the significator be under the earth,

that is, in either of the first six houses, it will be on the back or hinder part of the body. If only a few degrees of the sign ascend upon the horoscope, or descend on the sixth, or if the lord of the ascendant, lord of the sixth, or the moon be posited in the beginning of any sign, the said mole or mark will be found upon the upper part of the member those signs govern. If half the degrees of a sign ascend, or the significators are posited in the middle of any sign, the mole or mark will be in the middle of the member ; but if the last degrees of a sign ascend, or the significators are in the latter degrees of a sign, the mark or mole will be on the lower part of the member such sign governs.

PROGNOSTICATIONS BY MOLES.

IT is necessary to know the size of the mole, its colour, whether round, oblong, or angular ; because each will add to or diminish the force of the indication. The larger the mole, the greater the prosperity or adversity of the person ; the smaller the mole, the less his good or evil fate. If it is round, it indicates good ; if oblong, a moderate share of fortunate events ; if angular, a mixture of good and evil ; the deeper the colour the more it announces favour or disgrace ; the lighter, the less of either. If very hairy, much misfortune ; if few long hairs grow upon it, it denotes prosperity.

2.—A mole on the right side of the forehead or right temple, signifies sudden wealth and honour.

3.—A mole on the right eyebrow, denotes a speedy marriage with a person with amiable qualities and good fortune.

4.—A mole on the left of either of those three places, announces unexpected disappointment.

5.—A mole on the outside corner of either eye, denotes a person to be steady, sober, and sedate; but liable to a violent death.

6.—A mole on either cheek, signifies that the person will never rise above the mediocrity in fortune; though he will never fall into poverty.

7.—A mole on the nose, shows that the person will have good success in his undertakings.

8.—A mole on the lip, upper or lower, proves the person to be fond of delicate things, and much given to the pleasures of love, in which he or she will be successful.

9.—A mole on the chin, foreshows great prosperity, and high esteem.

10.—A mole on the side of the neck, shows that the person will narrowly escape suffocation, but will afterwards rise to great consideration by an unexpected legacy or inheritance.

11.—A mole on the throat, denotes that the person shall become rich by marriage.

12.—A mole on the right breast, denotes a sudden reverse from comfort to distress, by accidents. Most of his children will be girls.

13.—A mole on the left breast, signifies success in undertakings, and an amorous disposition. Most of his children will be boys.

14.—A mole on the bosom portends mediocrity of health and fortune.

15.—A mole under the left breast, over the heart, foreshows that a man will be of a warm disposition, unsettled in mind, fond of rambling, and light in his conduct. In a lady, sincerity in love, quick conception, and easy travail.

16.—A mole on the right side over the ribs, denotes a coward, and a person of dull understanding.

17.—A mole on the belly, denotes sloth, gluttony, selfishness, and slovenly in dress.

18.—A mole on either hip, denotes many children, and those that survive will be healthful, lusty, and patient in all hardships.

19.—A mole on the right thigh, denotes wealth, and success in marriage.

20.—A mole on the left thigh denotes much suffering from poverty and want of friends, as also by the enmity and injustice of others.

21.—A mole on the right knee, denotes good choice of a partner for life, and few disappointments.

22.—A mole on the left knee portends that the person will be rash, and inconsiderate, but modest when cool, honest, and of good behaviour.

23.—A mole on either leg shows that the person is indolent, thoughtless, and indifferent.

24.—A mole on either ancle denotes a man to be inclined to effeminacy and elegancy of dress—a lady, to be courageous, active, and industrious, with some spice of the termagant.

To give judgment upon the fate of any one, first examine the face of the heavens at the time of birth; secondly, judge the same by their whole assemblage of features, contained in the rules of physiognomy; thirdly, give judgment on the past, present, and future events of their lives, by the science of Palmistry; fourthly, by comparing your judgment in the above mentioned sciences with this prognostication of moles, see how they agree in respect to their several accounts, which are thus to be derived from them,

always remembering that the most votes will carry
the day.

PROGNOSTICATIONS BY CARDS.

The artist, after having obtained the true and full
meaning each card bears separately, and in its independent state, he must be able to form a judgment,
and vary all their mixtures, company, and combina-
tions, which are easily deducted, for these cards (like
planets, men, and other things,) are often altered
from their natural state by the company in which
they are found, which rule must be duly attended to.
Divination by cards is a kind of a geomantic lot,
always held in the highest repute by the ancients, who
would perform no important work without first consulting these lots; for whatever predictions of human
events are made in this way must have some sub-
lime occult cause, which shall not be a cause by
accident, as Aristotle describes fortune to be. No,
we must look higher, and find out a cause which
may intend the effect.

*It is no matter whether we make cards or anything
else the instrument with which we work in these high
mysteries;* therefore we must not place this in cor-
poreal nature, but in immaterial substances, which
administer the lot, even the signification of the truth;
as in men's souls or departed spirits, or in celestial
intelligences. That there is in man's soul sufficient
power to direct such kind of lots, is manifest, because
our souls have a divine virtue, apprehension and
power of all things, and all things have a natural
obedience to it, and so have a motion and efficacy to
that which the soul vehemently desires, when it is
carried to the excess of desire, and then all lots
assist the appetite of such a mind, and acquire won-

derful virtues of passages, as from that, so from the celestial opportunity in that hour in which the excess of such a like appetite doth most of all exceed in it.

And this is the foundation of all astrological and geomantic questions. The mind being thus elevated in any desire, taketh an hour and opportunity convenient and efficacious, on which the figure of the heavens being set, the artist may judge and plainly know concerning any subject, matter, or thing.

Therefore whatsoever kind of presage these lots portend, it cannot be made by mere chance, but from a spiritual cause, by virtue whereof the phantasy or hand of him that casteth the lot is moved, either by that power which proceeds from the soul of the operator, through the great excess of his affection, or from a celestial influence, or from a certain spirit assisting or moving from on high.

How to Divine by Cards.

First take a pack of cards and shuffle them well three times, making your significator which queen you please (if a lady performs the operations for herself, or king if a gentleman,) then lay them on the table nine in a row, and wherever you find yourself placed, count nine cards every way, not forgetting your said significator, and then you will see what card your significator comes in company with, and whatever it is, so it will happen to you.

If two red tens come against your said significator, it is a sign of marriage or prosperity; the ace of diamonds is a ring, the ace of hearts is your house, the ace of clubs is a letter, the ace of spades is death, or some grievous affliction, spite, or quarrelling (for that is the worst card in the pack.)

The ten of diamonds is a journey. The three of

hearts is a salute, the three of spades is tears, the ten of spades is sickness, the nine of spades is disappointment or trouble, the nine of clubs shows a jovial entertainment, the nine of hearts feasting, the ten of clubs travelling by water, the ten of hearts some place of amusement, the five of hearts a present, the five of clubs a bundle, the six of spades a child, the seven of spades a removal, the three of clubs fighting, the eight of clubs confusion, the eight of spades a road way, the four of clubs a strange bed, the nine of diamonds business, the five of diamonds a settlement, the five of spades a surprise, the two red eights new clothes, the three of diamonds speaking with a friend, the four of spades a sick bed, the seven of clubs a prison, the two of spades a false friend, the four of hearts a marriage-bed. If several diamonds come together, it is a sign that you will soon receive some money, several hearts, love, several clubs drink and noisy, troublesome company, and several spades, trouble and vexation.

If a married lady lay the cards, she must make her husband the king of the same suit she is queen of; but if a single lady use this science, she must make her lover what king she thinks proper; the knaves of the same suit are the men's thoughts, so they may know what they are thinking of, counting nine cards from where they are placed; and if any lady wishes to know whether she shall obtain her desires on any particular subject, let her shuffle the cards well, most earnestly wishing all the time for some one thing, she must then cut them once, particularly observing what card she cuts, then shuffle them again, and deal them out into three parcels, which done, look carefully over every parcel, and if that particular card you have just cut comes next yourself, or next the ace of hearts, you will have your wish, but if the nine of spades is next to you, you must then judge the contrary, as that is a disappointment; but you may try it three times, taking the major number of testimonies for a ground of your judgment.

CURIOUS GAMES WITH CARDS.

By which Fortunes are told in a singular and most diverting manner.

LOVERS' HEARTS.

FOUR young persons, but not more, may play at this game; or three, by making a dumb hand, or sleeping partner, as at whist. Play this game exactly the same in every game, making the queen, whom you call Venus, above ace, the aces in this game only standing for one, and hearts must be first led off by the person next the dealer. He or she who gets most tricks this way (each taking up their own, and no partnership) will have most lovers, and the king and queen of hearts in one hand shows matrimony at hand; but woe to the unlucky one that gets no tricks at the deal, or does not hold a heart in their hand; they will be unfortunate in love, and long tarry before they marry.

CUPID AND HYMEN.

THREE are enough for this game, the nines, the threes, and the aces; deal them equally; those who hold kings, hold friends; queens are rivals; knaves, shame; knave alone, lover; three, surprises; ace, sorrow; two together, shows a child before marriage; if a king alone is in her hand with the aces, she stands a good chance; but if a queen is with him, she will never marry the father; the nine of hearts gives the wish that you have most at heart; the nine of diamonds, money; and the nine of clubs, a new gown or coat; but the nine of spades is sorrow. A queen and a knave in one hand, bids fair for a secret intrigue.

HYMEN'S LOTTERY.

LET each one present deposit, as agreed on, some trifle; put a complete pack of cards, well shuffled, in a bag or reticule. Let the party stand in a circle, and the bag being handed round, each draw three. Pairs of any kind are favourable omens of good fortune to the party, and gets from the pool the sum back that each agreed to pay. The king of hearts is here made the god of love, and claims double, and gives a faithful swain to the fair one who has the good fortune to draw him: if Venus, the queen of hearts, is with him, it is the conquering prize, and clears the pool; fives and nines are reckoned crosses and misfortunes, and pay a forfeit of the sum agreed on to the pool, besides the usual stipend at each new game; three nines at one draw, shows the lady will be an old maid; three fives a bad husband.

MATRIMONY.

LET three, five, and seven youug women stand in a circle, and draw a card out of a bag; she who gets the highest card, will be married first, whether she be at the present time maid, wife, or widow; and she who has the lowest, has the longest time to stay till the wedding-day; she who draws the ace of spades will never bear the name of wife; and she who has the nine of hearts in this trial, will have one lover too many to her sorrow.

CUPID'S PASTIME.

BY this game you may amuse yourself and friends, and learn some curious particulars of your future fate. Several may play at the game, it requiring no number, only leaving out nine on their board, not exposed to view; each person puts a half-penny in the pool, and the dealer double. The ace of diamonds is made principal, and takes all the other aces, &c., like Pam at Loo; twos and threes in your hand are luck; fours a continuance in your present state; fives, troubles; sixes, profit; sevens, plague; eights, disappointment; nines, surprises; tens, settlement; knaves, sweethearts; kings and queens, friends and acquaintances; ace of spades, death; ace of clubs, a letter; and the ace of diamonds, with ten of hearts, marriage.

The ace of diamonds being played first, or if it be not cut, the dealer calls for the queen of hearts, which takes next; if the ace be not cut, and the queen conquers, the person who played her will marry that year, though unlikely at the time; but if she loses her queen, she must wait longer; the ace and queen being called, the rest go in rotation, as at whist, kings taking queens, queens knaves, and so on, and the more tricks you have, the more money you get off the board on the division after each game; those who hold the nine of spades, will soon have trouble, and they are to pay a penny to the board; but the fortunate fair one who holds the queen and knave of hearts in the same hand, will soon be married, or if already married, she will have a great rise in life by means of her husband; those who hold the ace of diamonds and queen of hearts, clear the money off the board, and end that game; it also betokens great prosperity.

DICE.

THIS is a certain and innocent way of finding out common occurences about to take place. Take three dice, shake them well in the box with your left hand, and then cast them out on a table, on which you had previously drawn a circle with chalk, but never throw on a Monday or Wednesday.

Three—a pleasing surprise.

Four—a disagreeable one.

Five—a stranger, who will prove a friend.

Six—loss of property.

Seven—undeserved scandal.

Eight—merited reproach.

Nine—a wedding.

Ten—a christening, at which some important event will occur to you.

Eleven—a death that concerns you.

Twelve—a letter, speedily.

Thirteen—tears and sighs.

Fourteen—a new admirer.

Fifteen—beware that you are not drawn into some trouble or plot.

Sixteen—a pleasant journey.

Seventeen—you will either be on the water, or have dealings with those belonging to it, to your advantage.

Eighteen—a great profit, rise in life, or some desirable good will happen immediately; for answers to dice are always fulfilled within nine days. To show the same number twice at one trial, shows news from abroad, whatever be the number. If the dice roll over the circle, the number thrown goes for nothing, but it shows sharp words, and if they fall to the floor, it is blows; in throwing out the dice, if one remains on the top of the other, it is a present, of which females must take care.

DOMINOES.

LAY them with their faces on the table, shuffle them, then draw one, and see the number.

DOUBLE-SIX—receiving a handsome sum of money.

SIX-FIVE—going to a public amusement.

SIX-FOUR—law-suits.

SIX-THREE—ride in a coach.

SIX-TWO—present of clothing.

SIX-ONE—you will soon perform a friendly action.

SIX-BLANK—guard against scandal, or you will suffer by your inattention.

DOUBLE-FIVE—a new abode to your advantage

FIVE-FOUR—a fortunate speculation.

FIVE-THREE—a visit from a superior

FIVE-TWO—a water party.

FIVE-ONE—a love intrigue.

FIVE-BLANK—a funeral, but not of a relation.

DOUBLE-FOUR—drinking liquor at a distance.

FOUR-THREE—a false alarm at your house.

FOUR-TWO—beware of thieves or swindlers. Ladies, notice this; it means more than it says.

FOUR-ONE—trouble from creditors.

FOUR-BLANK—a letter from an angry friend.

DOUBLE-THREE—sudden wedding, at which you will be vexed.

THREE-TWO—buy no lottery tickets, nor enter into any game of chance, or you will lose.

THREE-ONE—a great discovery at hand.

THREE-BLANK—an illegitimate child.

DOUBLE-TWO—plague by a jealous partner.

TWO-ONE—you will mortgage or pledge some property very soon.

DOUBLE-ONE—you will soon find something to your advantage in the street or road.

DOUBLE-BLANK—the worst presage in all the set of dominoes; you will soon have trouble from a quarter you little expect.

It is useless to draw more than three dominoes at one time, or in the same month, as they will deceive yourself; shuffle the dominoes each time of choosing; to draw a dominoe twice makes the answer stronger.

FORTUNATE DAYS, WEEKS, MONTHS, AND YEARS.

THE day of the week in which you were born, is the best; it is lucky to receive a letter on the third, fifth, or ninth of the month, or on a Tuesday or Saturday. The first week in May is fortunate for a new undertaking to men; the second to women. June is a good month, in which to contract, or receive promise of marriage, as it generally prospers.

It has often been recorded, and experience has shown it to be true, that some event of importance is sure to happen to a woman in her thirty-first year, whether single or married; it may prove for her good, or it may be some great evil or temptation; therefore, let her be cautious and circumspect in all her actions. If she is a maiden or a widow, it is probable that she marries this year. And so with men in their forty-second year; observe always, to grant or take a lease for an odd number of years; even are not prosperous. The three first days of the moon, are the best for signing papers; and the first five days, and the twenty-fourth, for any fresh undertaking. But it must be allowed that people's industry and perseverance often overcome a bad planet, or a day marked unlucky in the book of fate.

Mondays, Wednesdays, and Fridays, are the best for men; Tuesdays, Thursdays, and Saturdays, for women. To travel by land, choose the increase of the moon, the decrease for a voyage; and about the full to write letters in which you ask a favour; to beg wafers is not lucky on this occasion. It is not good to marry on your birth-day, for a woman, but it is fortunate for a man; it is good to christen a child on the day of the week in which it was born. It is fortunate to be born on a Sunday.

TRADITIONAL OBSERVATIONS.

It is not good for a maiden to marry in colours, or a widow in white; yet let her avoid green or yellow, and the thirteenth of the month.

To see a flight of birds as you go to the church on your nuptial day, foretells many children.

To meet a funeral is ominous at the time of speedy separation.

The sun to emerge suddenly from a cloud, and shine on the altar as the nuptials are celebrating, denotes prosperity and connubial love.

It is unlucky to pick up an odd glove in the street; you had better pass it.

Never tell a dream till you have broken your fast; if you have the same dream repeated twice or thrice, attend to it. it must have more than a common meaning.

TO KNOW YOUR HUSBAND'S TRADE.

Exactly at twelve, on Midsummer day, place a bowl of water in the sun, pour in some boiling pewter as the clock is striking, saying thus :—

> Here I try a potent spell
> Queen of love and Juno tell,
> In kind union to me,
> What my husband is to be ;
> This the day and this the hour,
> When it seems you have the power,
> For to be a maiden's friend,
> So, good ladies, condescend.

A tobacco-pipe full is enough. When the pewter is cold, take it out of the water, and dry it in a cloth, and you will find the emblems of your future husband's trade quite plain. If more than one, you will marry twice ; if confused and no emblems you will not marry ; a coach shows a gentleman for you.

———

CHARMS AND INCANTATIONS.

To be resorted to at certain seasons of the year, to procure by dreams an insight into futurity, particularly to marriage.

ST. AGNES' DAY

falls on the 21st of January ; prepare yourself by a twenty-four hours' fast, taking nothing but pure spring water, beginning at midnight on the 21st ; then go to bed, and sleep by yourself ; and do not mention what you are trying to any one or it will break the spell ; lie on your left side, and repeat these lines three times ;

St. Agnes be a friend to me,
In the gift I ask of thee;
Let me this night my husband see—

and you will dream of your future spouse; if you
see more men than one in your dream, you will wed
two or three times, but if you sleep and dream not,
you will never marry.

St. Magdalen.

LET three young women assemble together on the
eve of this saint in an upper apartment, where they
are sure not to be disturbed, and let no one try
whose age is more than 21, or it breaks the charm;
get rum, wine, gin, vinegar, and let each have a hand
in preparing the potion.

Put it in a ground glass vessel, for no other will
do; then let each dip a sprig of rosemary in, and
fasten it in her bosom, and taking three sips of the
mixture get into bed; and the three must sleep
together, but not a word must be spoken after the
ceremony begins, and you will have dreams of such
a nature that you cannot possibly mistake your
future destiny.

Magic Laurel.

RISE between three and four in the morning of
your birthday, so as to be observed by no one, and
pluck a sprig of laurel; convey it to your chamber,
and hold it over some lighted brimstone for five
minutes, wrap it in a white linen cloth or napkin,
together with your name written on paper, and that
of the young man who addresses you (or if more
than one, write all the names down), write also the
day of the week, the date of the year, and the age
of the moon; then haste and bury it in the ground,

where it must not be disturbed for three days and three nights; then take it up and place the parcel under your pillow for three nights, and your dreams will indicate your destiny.

A Spell.

MAKE a nosegay of various coloured flowers, one of a sort, a sprig of rue, and yarrow off a grave, and bind all together with the hair of your head; sprinkle them with a few drops of the oil of amber, using your left hand, and bind the flowers round your head when you retire to rest under your night-cap; put on clean sheets and linen, and your fate will appear in your dream.

The Three Keys.

PURCHASE three small keys, each at a different place, and going to bed tie them together with your garter, and place them in your left hand glove, with a small flat dough cake, on which you have pricked the first letters of your sweetheart's name; put them in your bosom when you retire to rest; if you are to have that young man you will dream of him, but not else.

Promise of Marriage.

IF you receive a written declaration to that effect in a letter, prick the words with a needle on a sheet of paper clear from any writing; fold it in nine folds, and place it under your head when you go to rest. If you dream of diamonds, castles, or a clear sky, there is no deceit, and you will prosper; trees in blossom, or flowers, show children; washing, or graves, show you will lose them by death; and water shows they are faithful, but you will go through severe poverty with the party for some time though all may end well.

STRANGE BED.

LAY under your pillow a prayer-book opened at the matrimonial service, bound round with the garters you wore that day, and a sprig of myrtle on the page that says, *with this ring I thee wed*, and your dream will be ominous.

ACORNS.

TRY on the third day of the month between September and March. Let any number of young women not excecding nine, and minding that there is an odd one in the company, and each string nine acorns on a separate string, or as many acorns as there are females, but not more; wrap them round a long stick of wood, and place it in the fire, just as the clock strikes twelve at night; say not a word, but sit round the fire till all the acorns are consumed, then take out the ashes, and retire to bed almost directly, repeating:

> May love and marriage be the theme,
> To visit me in this night's dream;
> Gentle Venus, be my friend,
> The image of my lover send;
> Let me see his form and face,
> By a symbol or a sign,
> Cupid, forward my design.

A CHRISTMAS SPELL.

STEEP nine mistletoe berries in a mixture of ale wine, vinegar, and honey; take them on going to bed, and you will dream of your future lot; a storm in this dream is very bad; it is likely you will marry a sailor who will suffer shipwreck; but to see either sun, moon, or stars, is a good presage; so are flowers; but a coffin, disappointment in love.

VALENTINE.

IF you receive one, and cannot guess the party who sent it, or are in doubt; prick the fourth finger of your left hand, and with a crow-quill write on the back of the valentine the day, hour, and year of your birth, also the present year, the moon's age, and the name of the present morning-star, all which you will find in the almanack, and the sign into which the sun has entered; try this on the first Friday after you receive the valentine, but do not go to bed till midnight; place the paper in your left shoe, and put it under your pillow; lay on your left side, and repeat three times:—

> St. Valentine, pray condescend
> To be this night a maiden's friend;
> Let me now my lover see
> Be he of high or low degree;
> By a sign his station show,
> Be it weal or be it woe,
> Let him come to my bed side,
> And my fortune thus decide.

The young woman will be sure to dream of the identical person who sent the valentine, and may guess by the other particulars of the dream, if or not he is to be her spouse.

A LENT CHARM.

To be tried on any Friday in Lent, Good Friday excepted, when it is improper to try anything of the kind. Write twelve letters of the alphabet on separate pieces of card, also twelve figures, and the same number of blank cards, then put them in a bag and shake them well, and let each present draw one; a blank shows a single life; a figure, intrigue, or crim. con.; a letter, a happy marriage.

YARROW.

This is a weed commonly found in abundance on graves, towards the close of the spring and beginning of the summer. It must be plucked exactly on the first hour of morn; place three sprigs either in your shoe or glove saying:—

> Good morning, good morning, good yarrow,
> And thrice a good morning to thee;
> Tell me before this time to-morrow,
> Who my true love is to be.

A young man must pluck the weed off a young maiden's grave, and a female select that of a bachelor's; retire to bed without speaking another word, as it dissolves the spell; put the yarrow under your pillow, and it will procure a dream on which you may depend.

A CHARM,

to be used on the eve of any fast-day. This takes a week's preparation, for you must abstain from meat or strong drink; go not to bed till the clock has struck the midnight hour, and rise before seven the next morning, the whole seven days; you must not play at cards, or any other game of chance, nor enter any place of public diversion; when you go to bed on the night of trial eat something very salt, and do not drink after it, and you may depend on having singular dreams, and being thirsty you may dream of liquids; wine is excellent, and shows wealth; brandy, foreign land; rum, that you will wed a sailor; gin, but a middling life; cordials, variety of fortune; and water, if you drink it, poverty; but to see a clear

stream is good. Children are not good to behold in
this dream ; cards and dice forebode the loss of reputation, or that you will never marry.

TO CAST NATIVITIES.

ASCERTAIN the exact time and the hour in which
you were born, procure a Moore's almanack of that
year, to direct you to the sign that then reigned, the
name of the planets, and the state of the moon ; observe whether the sun was just entering the sign,
whether it was near the end, or what was its particular
progress ; if at the beginning, your fate will be strongly
tinctured with its proper ties, moderate at the meridian, and slightly if the sun is nearly going out of
the sign ; then judge of the planets by the introduc-
tion of the book. Write down the day of the week,
see whether it is a lucky day or not, the state of the
moon, the nature of the planets, and the influence
described next, and you will ascertain your future
destiny with very little trouble.

JANUARY.—*Aquarius, or the Water Bearer,*

gives a love of wandering and variety, seldom contented long in one place, or supposed injuries ; soon
affronted, slow to forgive ; fond of law. Mercury
gives slights in love. A full moon is the best, for a
new moon only adds to their false fears ; and Saturn
gives them trouble to contend with.

FEBRUARY.—*Pisces, or the Fishes.*

Those born under it, prosper best on the ocean, or
at a distance from their native home. But if not
ordained to travel, they will sometimes experience
distress ; Mars and Jupiter are the best planets. If

the day of the week on which they were born be a
fortunate one, let them begin their fresh concerns,
write and answer letters, or seek for money due to
them, and they will succeed. The female traveller
will be very fortunate, and despise danger, yet neither
her disposition nor manners will be masculine; she
will make an excellent wife and mother, and if left a
widow with children, will strive for their interest with
a father's care and prudence, nor will she wed a
second time unless Venus rules her destiny; Mars
gives her success; Jupiter, vigilance; a new moon,
virtue; a full moon, some enemies; and Saturn, temptation; and yet she will prosper.

MARCH.—*Aries, or the Ram.*

A very good sign to those born under it, denoting
prosperity, fidelity, dutiful children, and many liberal
friends, but hot-tempered; if Mercury is one of the
planets, they will then be very amiable. Jupiter and
Venus are also good planets to them; but Mars or
Saturn causes a sad alteration to their general destiny,
and gives a mixed life of pain and pleasure. Venus
reigning alone as a morning star at the time of their
birth, causes them many amours.

APRIL.—*Taurus, or the Bull.*

To be prosperous under this sign will require active
industry and patience under misfortunes and perils;
but Jupiter, Venus, or the new moon, will soften this
destiny. The man will be bold and adventurous, fond
of governing, and hard to please; they must be careful not to enter on any fresh concern while their sign
has the ascendancy, the end of April and the two
first weeks in May.

MAY.—*Gemini, or the Twins.*

Very fortunate for females, particularly in matrimony, though they will prosper well in other affairs: the full moon and Venus good for them. They will be punctual and honest in their dealings, be much respected by their friends and neighbours, and have many children.

JUNE.—*Cancer, or the Crab.*

An eventful sign to both sexes, but particularly to those of a fair complexion; they will be exalted in life—Jupiter and Venus are the best signs for them; but the brunettes, though fortunate, will plague themselves and others with whims, jealousies, and ill nature. If Mars be their planet, they will enter into law-suits; and if Saturn, let them beware of ungovernable passions.

JULY.—*Leo, or the Lion.*

Favourable to those born in poverty, but not to the rich; for this sign shows a great change of circumstances about the meridian of your days; sooner or later, according to the time of the sign in which you were born. If Jupiter be the planet, the person born poor will become rich by legacies, or will marry their master or mistress, or his or her son or daughter, according to their sex; and a happy life.

AUGUST.—*Virgo, or the Virgin.*

A most important sign; the men brave, generous, candid, and honest; the females amiable and prosperous, if they mar not their fortune by love of flattery, or advancement awaits them. Venus is not a good planet for them, and Saturn shows seduction; but if neither of them predominate at their birth, they will marry early, have good children, and enjoy the most valuable blessings of life, and have many unexpected gains.

September.—*Libra, or the Balance.*

A middle course of life is promised by this sign; free from storms or sudden changes, in fact, an enviable destiny. The persons now born will be just in their transactions, faithful in love and wedlock, and averse to law; not many children, but those healthy.

October.—*Scorpio, or the Scorpion.*

To the man, promises a long, active, useful life, and an intelligent mind; prosperous, and very careful of what he gains; a good husband, parent, and master, and a sincere friend; gay in his youthful days, but not vicious. Jupiter and a full moon adds to the good of his destiny; Saturn or Mercury will detract from it; Venus inclines him to the fair sex. To the woman, it shows indolence; and, if prosperous, it will not be by her own merit or industry; for she will have to thank those to whom she is nearly allied; but if she has no shining qualities prominent, she will be free from evil propensities, and will never bring disgrace on herself, her husband, her family, or friends, unless Venus reigned at her birth; no other planet will affect her destiny.

November.—*Sagittarius, or the Archer.*

Gives to both sexes an amorous disposition; and if Venus or Mercury presides at their birth, they will love variety; Jupiter and Mars are good for them; the new moon is excellent to the female, and full to the man. Persons born on this sign seldom marry, if the first-mentioned planets reign; or if they do, it is late in life, or when the meridian of their days is over, and they are become wise to relinquish folly, they then become steady and prudent, and generally do well; they seldom have many children, but what they have will prosper, and have friends to promote their interest.

December.—*Capricorn, or the Goat.*

Shows you will work and toil, and others reap the benefit of your labour, unless marriage alters the destiny; but hard will be your fate if your spouse is of the same sign, but if Jupiter be a planet at your birth, the end of your days will be prosperous. A woman may probably better her fate by a second marriage, especially if Venus be her planet.

THE WAY TO GET RICH.

And Live Happy in the Marriage State.

"There is a tide in the affairs of man, which if taken at the ebb will lead to fortune."

> He that by the plough would thrive,
> Himself must either hold or drive,
> For age and want save while you may,
> No morning sun lasts a whole day:
> Get what you can, and what you get, hold,
> 'Tis a stone that will turn all your lead to gold.
> Therefore be ruled by me, I pray,
> Save something for a rainy day.

Remember, that time is money, for he that can earn ten shillings a day at his labour, and goes abroad, or sits idle at home, one half of that day, though he spend but sixpence during his diversion, or idleness, he ought not to reckon that the only expense; he hath really wasted, or rather thrown away five shillings, besides.

Remember, that credit is money; if a man let his money remain in my hands after it is due, because he has a good opinion of my credit, he gives me the interest, or as much as I can make of the money during that time; this amounts to a considerable sum, where a man hath large credit, and makes good use of it.

Remember, that money is of a multiplying nature; money will produce money, and its offspring will produce more; and so five shillings turned is six, being turned again is seven and threepence, and so on, till it becomes a hundred pounds; and the more there is of it, the more it will produce on every turning, so that the profits rise quicker and quicker; and he who throws away a crown, destroys all that it might have produced, even scores of pounds.

Remember, that six pounds a year is but a groat a day for this little sum (which may be wasted either in time or expenses unperceived); which, on the contrary, if a proper use be made of the same, he may, on his own security, have the constant possession and use of an hundred and twenty pounds. So much in stock, briskly turned, will always produce the greatest advantage to the tradesman. Remember that the good pay-master is lord of another man's purse, for he who pays punctually at the time he promises, may, at any time, raise all the money his friend can spare. Next to industry and frugality, nothing can contribute more to the raising of a man in the world than punctuality in all his dealings. Therefore, never keep borrowed money one hour beyond the time promised, lest the disappointment

shut up your friend's purse for ever, as the most
trifling actions that affect a man's credit ought
always to be avoided. The sound of the hammer at
five in the morning, or at nine at night, heard by a
creditor, makes him easy six months longer;—but if
he sees you at a gaming-table, or in a tavern when
you should be at work, he sends for his money the
very next day, and demands it before it is convenient for you to pay him.

Beware of thinking all your own that you possess,
and of living accordingly; this is a mistake that
many people of credit fall into—to prevent this,
always keep an exact daily account of your expenses
and daily income and profits (which hath been my
daily practice for these last twenty years, and I have
always found the good effects of the same). For if
you will just take the trouble at first to enumerate
particulars, it will discover how small trifling
expenses mount up to a large sum; by which you
will see what might have been, and also what may
for the future be saved, without causing any great
inconvenience. In short, the way to obtain riches, is
as plain as the way to market, which depends chiefly
on two things, viz., industry and frugality; and take
care that you waste neither time nor money, but
daily make the best use of both; if you take care
of the hours and days, the weeks, months, and years,
will take care of themselves.

I have always found that any business being first
well contrived, is more than half done; for a sleeping fox catches no poultry; there will be sleeping
enough in the grave; and, also, that lost time is but
seldom found again, for that which we call time
enough, generally proves little enough; for sloth
makes things difficult, while industry makes them

easy. He that rises late, must trot hard all day,
and shall scarce overtake his business at night—for
laziness travels so slow that poverty soon overtakes
him.   Drive your business, but let that not drive
you ; for early to bed and early to rise, is the way
to become healthy, wealthy, aud wise.   Industry need
not wish—while he who lives on a vain hope, will
die fasting, for there is nothing to be done or
accomplished under the sun without labour.   He
that hath a trade hath an estate, and he that hath
a profession, hath an office and profit with honour ;
but then the trade must be worked at, and the profession well followed, or they will not enable you to
pay rent and taxes.   For, at the working man's
house, hunger looks in, but dares not enter ; for
industry pays debts, while despair increases them.
Diligence is the mother of good luck, as Solomon
saith, *the diligent hand maketh rich, while he that deal-
eth with a slack hand becometh poor ;* for God gives
all things to industry.   *Then plough deep, while slug-
gards sleep,* and you shall have plenty, while others
complain of hard times.

Keep working while it is called to-day, for you do
not know how much you may be hindered to-morrow ;
and never leave that business to be done to-morrow
which you can do to-day ; for since you are not
sure of a single hour, throw not that away.   How
many are there who daily live by their wits, and
who often break from want of a stock in hand—
while industry gives comfort, plenty, and respect.
Keep your shop well, and then your shop will keep
you.   For it sometimes happens that the eye of a
master will do more work than both his hands ; and
more especially if his head be of any reasonable
length, for the want of care generally doth more

damage than the want of knowledge. If you do not overlook your workmen, you may just as well leave them your purse open; for trusting too much to the care of others has ruined many a man; for if you would be wealthy, think of being careful and saving; for

> "Woman, wine, game, and deceit,
> Make the wealth small, and the wants great."

For all that which maintains one vice, would bring up two children. If you wish to know the value of money, just go and try to borrow a little; for he that goes a borrowing goes a sorrowing, and so doth he who lends it unto such people, when he tries to get it back again; for pride that dines on vanity, sups on content, and often breakfasts with plenty, dines with poverty, and sups with infamy, creates envy, and hastens misfortunes, for it is hard for an empty bag to stand upright.—Creditors have generally much better memories than debtors, who are also a kind of superstitious sect, great observers of set or appointed days and times; so that those have but a short Lent who owe money to be paid at Easter; for expenses are always so constant and certain, that it is much easier to build two chimneys than to keep one in fuel; rather to go to bed supperless than to rise in debt; for to always do unto others as you would wish to be done by, is the first fundamental law of natural justice.

DIVINATION BY BIRDS AND BEASTS.

It hath been observed by the learned in all ages, that our all-wise and beneficent Creator originally implanted in the frame of nature, a means whereby mankind may attain to the knowledge of such future contingencies as concern their happiness ; and especially, since we observe that even the most inconsiderate creatures are more or less endowed with a gift of fore-knowledge. Thus the industrious bee, and laborious ant, lay in their summer store to supply their necessary wants in winter ; yea, of the whole race of reptiles, the ant, the spider, and bee, appear to be endowed with the greatest sagacity.

The wisdom of ants is conspicuous in forming themselves into a kind of republic, and therein observing their own peculiar laws and policies ; but the cunning of the spider exceeds that of most other insects ; its various artifices to ensnare its prey, are no less remarkable than its contrivance of a cell or retreat behind its web, where it feasts upon its game in safety, and conceals the fragments of those carcases it has devoured, without exposing the least remains of its barbarity, which might distinguish its place of abode. Into what history can we look, to find people governed by laws equal to those in the republic of bees? What experience can we desire beyond that of the cunning spider, to teach us to guard against those who lay snares to catch the unwary ? or what can exceed the indefatigable ant, in teaching frugality and industry ?

The badger, hedge-hog, and mole, also provide a magazine of plants and herbs, tu enable them to lie safely concealed in their holes during the frosts of winter. Their holes are constructed with great art, and have generally two apertures, that, when beset by an enemy, they may escape by the other. The doublings of the hare, and the tricks of the fox, to escape the hounds, are also astonishing indications of foresight and sagacity. The feathered race are also endowed with a similar faculty, and often foretell an approaching storm a considerable time before it ap- apears by retiring in flocks to their hiding-places for shelter and protection. This is the case especially with birds of passage, for they assemble in prodigious flocks at an appointed hour, and leave before the approach of winter; which they foresee will destroy the flies and insects, on which they feed. And it is extraordinary that these birds return as early as the sun brings this class of insects into new life, and they find out and possess their old nests.

The wise forecast for self-preservation and safety is even extended to the innumerable inhabitants of the immense ocean, where the fishes pressed by hunger, indiscriminately prey upon one another, the large upon the small, even of its own species; whence the smaller fish, when in danger of being devoured, fly to the shallow waters, where their enemy either can- not or dare not pursue them. And this pursuit is not confined to a single region, for it is the case from the vicinity of the pole down to the equator; thus the cod from the banks of Newfoundland pur- sues the whiting even to the northern shores of Spain. It is astonishing also that herrings, which appear to generate towards the north of Scotland, regularly make their way once a year to the British Channel. Their voyage is conducted with the utmost regularity, and the time of their departure is fixed from the month of June to August. They always assemble together before they set out, and no strag- glers are ever found from the general body. It is impossible to assign any cause for this emigration, but the same instinctive impulse with which all orders of animated nature are more or less endued.

Observe, when you go out of your house to do any kind of business, and in the way you see a man, or a bird going or flying, so that either of them set themselves before you on your right hand, that is a good sign for your business; but when you see a bird or man before you on the left side of you, it is an ill sign in reference to your business. When either a man or a bird pass before you, coming from the right side of you, and bending towards the left, goeth out of your sight, that is a good sign concerning your business. When you first find a man going, or a bird flying, and then rests himself before you on your right side, and you seeing it, it is a sign of success in your business.

When you see a man or a bird bending from your right side, to the left, it is an ill sign for your business; when they come behind you, and go faster than you, but before coming up they rest, or the same before you come to them, on your right side, it is a good sign. But if on the left side, it is an evil sign. A man or a bird coming from your left side to the right, goeth out of your sight without resting, it is a good sign. If a man or a bird coming from your right hand, behind you to the left, and resting any where, is an evil sign. The signs which happen in the beginning of any business must be noticed. In the beginning of any work, if rats have been gnawing your clothes, then desist from your undertakings. If at going out of your house, you stumble on the threshold, or in the way you stumble against any thing, then forbear your journey; if any ill omen happens at the beginning of your business, put it off for awhile, lest you be disappointed.

If a crow, raven, or a jackdaw croak over any

person, it shows evil of a serious nature. The magpie denotes you will soon hear news, and come into company; but whether such news be good or bad, observe whether it comes from the right hand or the left. The screech owl is always unfortunate, for, about the 17th of Oct., 1807, Grantham church was a repository for owls every evening, for one month, when it followed, that before that time the next year, it was actually robbed of all its plate and money, to a large amount, by a gang of villains, in the dead of the night, to the great loss of the parish. If you meet sparrows, it is unfortunate, except for love. Flies indicate importunity and impudent affronts; cocks meeting you, or crowding against your house, inform you of visitors, and success in your journeys and business. If you meet a hare, a mule, or a hog, it is an ill omen; to meet horses in a carriage is good, but if you meet an ass, expect trouble; to meet sheep and goats indicates prosperity in your affairs; if you meet a dog or oxen, it is good; mice indicate you will soon meet with danger; locusts making a stand in any place, is an ill omen; grasshoppers promote a journey, and foretell good events.

The spider weaving a line downward, signifies money to come; ants having a nest near your door is good, because they know how to provide for themselves, and portend security and riches. If you meet with a snake, take care of an ill-tongued enemy: a viper signifies lewd women and wicked children; an eel shows a man displeased with every body. But of all the various omens, none are more effectual or potent than man, that signify the truth more clearly. Therefore, diligently note the condition of that man you meet, or who meeteth you; his age, profession, station, gesture, motion, exercise, complexion, habit, name, words, speech, &c.; for, as there are in all animals so many discoveries of presages, yet those are all more efficacious and clear, which are infused into the soul of man. We must also consider what animals are Saturnine, or under Jupiter, Mars, &c., and according to their properties, draw forth their presages. Appollonius, of Tyanea, well understood the language of birds, as it is certain they have a peculiar language of their own as well as all the beasts of the field.

RULES TO KNOW THE TEMPER

AND DISPOSITION OF EVERY ONE.

The Signs of a Choleric Disposition, are

1.—The habit of the body hot in touch, dry, lean, hard, and hairy.

2.—The colour of the face yellow.

3.—A natural dryness of the mouth and tongue.

4.—The thirst great and frequent.

5.—Activity and inquietude of the body.

6.—The pulse hard, swift, and often beating.

7.—The spittle bitter.

8.—The dreams are most of yellow things, of brawls, of fights, and quarrels.

The signs of a Sanguine Constitution, are

1.—The habit of the body hot in touch, fleshy, soft, and hairy.

2.—The colour of the body fresh, sanguine, and lively.

3.—A natural and constant blush in the face.

4.—The pulse soft, moist, and full.

5.—The sweetness of the spittle.

6.—Dreams most commonly of red things, of beauty, feasting, dancing, music, and all jovial and pleasing recreations.

7.—A continual habit of pleasantness, affability.

8.—Often given to jests, mirth, and laughter.

The signs of a Phlegmatic Constitution, are

1.—The habit of the body cold and moist, in touch soft, fat, gross, and not hairy.

2.—A constant natural wanness in the face.

3.—The pulse soft, slow and rare.

4.—The thirst little, seldom desiring drink.

5.—The dreams usually of white things, floods, inundations, and accidents by water.

6.—Sleep, much and frequent.

7.—Slowness of the body to exercise.

The signs of a Melancholy Constitution, are

1.—The body in touch cold, dry, smooth.

2.—The body of a dark, dull, leaden colour.

3.—The spittle in little quantity, and sour.

4.—Pulse little, rare, and hard.

5.—The dreams often of black and terrible things —of spirits, ghosts, dreadful apprehensions, choaking, and beheading; mad beasts, as wolves, and tigers, ready to devour you.

6.—Greatly oppressed with fear.

7.—A stability in cogitations, and constancy in the performance of the thing intended.

The Physiognomical Signs of a good Genius, are

A straight erect body, neither over tall nor short, between fat and thin, the flesh naturally soft, the skin neither soft nor rough, but a medium ; the complexion white, verging to a blush of redness, the hair between hard and soft, usually of a brown colour, the head and face of a moderate size, the forehead rather high, the eyes manly, big, and clear, of a blue or hazel colour, the aspect mild and humane, the teeth are so mixed, that some are broad and some are narrow, a subtle tongue, and the voice between intense and remiss, the neck comely and smooth, the channel-bone of the throat appearing and moving, the back and ribs not over fleshy, the shoulders plain and slender, the hands indifferently long and smooth, the fingers long, smooth, and equally distant, the nails white, mixed with red, and shining, and the carriage of the body erect in walking.

CHARMS AND CEREMONIES.

To See a Future Husband.

On Midsummer eve, just after sunset, three, five, or seven young women are to go into a garden, in which is no other person, and each to gather a sprig of red sage, and then going into a room alone, set a stool in the middle of a room, and on it a bason full of rose-water, in which put the sprigs of sage, tying a line across the room, on one side of the stool, each woman is to hang on it a clean shift, turned the wrong side outwards ; then all are to sit down in a row, on the opposite side of the stool, as far distant as the room will admit, not speaking a word the whole time, whatever they see, and in a few minutes after twelve, each one's future husband will take her sprig out of the rose-water, and sprinkle her shift with it.

On St. Agnes' night, the 21st January, take a row of pins, and pull all out one by one, saying a paternoster on sticking a pin in your sleeve, and you will dream of him you will marry.

A slice of bride cake three times drawn through a wedding-ring, and laid under the head of an unmarried woman, will make her dream of her future husband. The same is practised in the north with a piece of the groaning cheese.

To see a future spouse in a dream; the party must lie in a different county from that in which they reside, and on going to bed, must knit the left gartar about the right-legged stocking, letting the other garter and stocking alone; and as they rehearse this verse, at every comma knit a knot:—

> This knot I knit, to know the thing I know not yet,
> That I may see the man that shall my husband be,
>   How he goes, and what he wears,
>   And what he does all days and years.

Accordingly, in a dream he will appear, with the insignia of his trade or profession.

Another, performed by charming the moon:—at the first appearance of the new moon after the new year's day, go out in the evening, and stand over the spears of the gate or stile, and, looking on the moon repeat the following lines:—

> All hail to thee, moon! all hail to thee!
> I pr'ythee, good moon, reveal to me
> This night, who my husband must be.

And you will then dream of your future husband.

To know the Fortune of your Future Husband.

Take a walnut, a hazel-nut, and nutmeg; grate them together, and mix them with butter and sugar, and make them into small pills, of which nine must be taken on going to bed; and you will dream of the state of the person you will marry. If a gentleman, of riches; if a clergyman, of white linen; if a lawyer, of darkness; if a tradesman, of noises and tumults; if a soldier or sailor, of thunder and lightning; if a servant, of rain.

CHARMS, SPELLS, AND INCANTATIONS.

To be used on particular Eves of Fasts and Festivals, to procure Dreams, Tokens, and other Insights into Futurity.

FAST OF ST. ANNE'S.

THIS is a hard trial, but what is not impossible to any young lady who wishes to know her lot in marriage. Prepare yourself three days previous to the eve of this female saint, by living on bread and water and parsley, and touch no other thing whatever, or your labour will be lost; the eve begins at the sixth hour. Go to bed as soon as you once begin to undress; get into bed, lay on your left side with your head as low as possible, then repeat the following verse three times :—

> St. Anne, in silver clouds descend,
> Prove thyself a maiden's friend;
> Be it good, or be it harm,
> Let me have knowledge from the charm;
> Be it husbands, one, two, three,
> Let me in rotation see;

And if fate decrees me four,
(No British maid can wish for more,)
Let me view them in my dream,
Fair and clearly to be seen;
But if the stars decree
Perpetual virginity,
Let me sleep on, and dreaming not,
I shall know my single lot.

THE MAGIC ROSE.

Gather your rose on the 27th of June, let it be
full blown, and as bright a red as you can get;
pluck it between the hours of three and four in the
morning, taking care none see you; convey it to
your chamber, and hold it over a chafing-dish, or any
convenient utensil, in which there are charcoal and
sulphur of brimstone, hold your rose over the smoke
about five minutes, and it will have a wonderful
effect on the flower.   Immediately put it in a sheet
of paper, on which is written your name and that of
the young man you love best; also the date of the
year, and the name of the morning star that has then
the ascendancy; fold it up, and seal it with three
separate seals, then bury the parcel at the foot of
the tree from which you gathered the flower; let it
remain untouched till the sixth of July, take it up at
midnight, go to bed and place it under your pillow,
and you will have a most eventful dream. You may
keep the rose under your head three nights without
spoiling the charm.

HOW TO MAKE THE DUMB-CAKE.

Let any number of young women take a handful
of wheaten flour, (and from the moment the hand
touches the flour, not a word is to be spoken during
the process,) and place it on a sheet of white paper,
then sprinkle it over with as much salt as can be

held betwixt the finger and thumb; then one of the damsels must bestow as much of her own water as will make it into dough; which being done, each of the company must roll it up, and spread it thin and broad; and each person must at some distance from each other, make the first letters of her Christian and surname, with a large new pin towards the end of the cake (if more Christian names than one, the first letter of each must be made;) the cake must be then set before the fire, and each person must sit in a chair, as distant as possible from the fire, not speaking a word all this while.

This must be done soon after eleven at night, and between that and twelve each person must turn the cake once, and in a few minutes after twelve, the husband of her to be first married will appear to lay his hand on that part of the cake marked with her name.

To FIND OUT THE FIRST TWO LETTERS OF A FUTURE WIFE'S OR HUSBAND'S NAME.

TAKE a small Bible and the key of your front street-door, and open to Solomon's Songs, ch. viii. ver. 6 and 7, place the wards of the key on those two verses, and let the bow of the key be about an inch out of the top of the Bible; shut the book, and tie it round with your garter, so as the key will not move, and the person who wishes to know his or her future husband or wife's signature, must suspend the Bible, by putting the middle finger of the right hand under the bow of the key, and the other person in like manner on the other side of the bow of the key, who must repeat the following verses, after the other person's saying the alphabet, one letter to each time repeating them. Mention to the person who repeats the verses, before you begin, which you intend to try first, whether surname or Christian name; and hold the Bible steady, and when you arrive at the appointed letter, the book will turn round under your finger, and that you will find to be the first letter of your intended's name.

Solomon's Songs, chap. viii. ver. 6 and 7.

"Set me as a seal upon thine heart, as a seal upon thine arm; for love is strong as death; jealousy is cruel as the grave, the coals thereof are coals of fire, which hath a most vehement flame.

"Many waters cannot quench love, neither can the floods drown it; if a man would give all the substance of his house for love, it would be utterly contemned."

To know how soon You will be Married.

GET a green pea-pod, in which are exactly nine peas; hang it over the door, and then take notice of the next person who comes in, who is not of the family, and if it proves a bachelor, you will certainly be married within that year.

On any Friday, take rosemary flowers, bay leaves, thyme, and sweet marjoram, of each a handful; dry these and make them into a fine powder; then take a tea-spoonful of each sort, mix the powders together; then take twice the quantity of barley flour and make the whole into a cake with the milk of a red cow. This cake is not to be baked, but wrapped in clean writing-paper, and laid under your head any Friday night. If the person dreams of music, she will shortly wed those she desires; if of fire, she will be crossed in love; if of a church, she will die single. If anything is written or the least spot of ink is on the paper it will not do.

To know if any One shall enjoy their Love or not.

TAKE the number of the first letter of your name, the number of the planet, and the day of the week; put all these together, and divide them by thirty; if it be above, it will come to your mind, and if below, to the contrary; and mind that number which exceeds not thirty.

To know if a Child New-born will live.

WRITE the proper names of the father and of the mother, and of the day the child was born, and put to each letter its number, as you did before, and unto the total sum, being collected together, put twenty-five, and divide the whole by seven; if it be even, the child will die; but if it be uneven, the child will live.

To know if a Woman with Child will have a Girl or a Boy.

WRITE the proper names of the father and the mother, and of the month she conceived with child, and likewise adding all the numbers of those letters together, divide them by seven; and then, if the remainder be even, it will be a girl, if uneven it will be a boy.

The Nine Keys.

GET nine small keys of your own, (borrowing will not do, nor must you tell what you want them for); plait a three-plaited band of your own hair, and tie them together, fastening the ends with nine knots; fasten them with one of your garters to your left wrist on going to bed, and bind the other garter round your head; then say,

St. Peter, take it not amiss,
To try your favour I've done this;
You are the ruler of the keys,
Favour me then if you please;
Let me then your influence prove,
And see my dear and wedded love.

This must be done on the eve of St. Peter's; it is
an old charm used by the maidens of Rome in ancient
times, who put great faith in it.

THE MYSTERIOUS WATCH.

REQUEST any person to lend you his watch, and
ask him if it will go when laid on the table. He
will, no doubt, answer in the affirmative; then place
it over the concealed magnet, and it will stop. Then
mark the precise spot where you placed the watch,
and moving the point of the magnet, give the watch
to another person, and desire him to make the experiment; in which he not succeeding, give it to a third
(replacing the magnet), and he will immediately perform it to the chagrin of the second party.

This experiment cannot be effected, unless you use
a very strongly impregnated magnetic bar, and that
the balance wheel of the watch be of steel, which may
be ascertained by previously opening it, and looking
at the works.

THE WITCHES' CHAIN.

LET three young women join in making a long
chain, a yard long, of Christmas juniper, and mistletoe berries, and at the end of every link put an oak
acorn. Exactly before midnight let them assemble
in a room by themselves where no one can disturb
them; leave a window open, and take the key out
of the key-hole and hang it over the chimney-piece;
have a good fire, and place in the midst of it a long

thinnish log of wood, well sprinkled with oil, salt, and fresh mould, then wrap the chain round it, each maiden having an equal share in the business; then sit down, and on your left knee let each fair one have a prayer-book opened at the matrimonial service. Just as the last acorn is burnt, the future husband will cross the room; each will see her own proper spouse, but he will be invisible to the wakeful virgins. Those that are not to wed will see a coffin, or some misshapen form, cross the room; go to bed and you will have remarkable dreams. This must be done only on a Wednesday or Friday night.

LOVE-LETTERS.

ON receiving a love-letter that has any particular declaration in it, lay it wide open; then fold it in nine folds, pin it next to your heart, till bed-time; then place it in your left hand glove, and lay it under your head. If you dream of gold, diamonds, or any other costly gem, your lover is true, and means what he says; if of white linen, you will lose him by death; and if of flowers, he prove false. If you dream of his saluting you, he is at present false, and means not what he professes, but only to draw you into a snare.

TO RECEIVE ORACLES BY DREAMS.

I CALL that a dream which proceeds either from the spirit of the phantasy and intellect united together, or by the illustration of the agent intellect above our souls, or by the true revelation of some divine power in a quiet and purified mind; for by this our soul receives true oracles, and abundantly

yields prophecies to us; as in dreams we seem both
to ask questions, and learn to find them out. Also
many doubtful things, many policies, many things
unknown, unwished for, and never attempted by our
minds, are manifested to us in dreams; also things
unknown, and unknown places, appear to us, and the
images of men alive and dead: and things to come
are foretold, and those which have happened are
revealed, which we know not by report. Such
dreams need not any art of interpretation, as those
which belong to divination, not to fore-knowledge;
for they who have such dreams understand them
not; for, dreams arise from the strength of imagination, to understand them from the strength of understanding.

He whose intellect is overwhelmed by too much
commerce with the flesh, is in a deep sleep, or fan-
tastic power, or his spirit is dull and unpolished, so
that it cannot receive the seals, &c. Now those who
desire to receive oracles by a dream, let them make
a ring of the Sun for this purpose. There are also
images of dreams, which being put under the head
when he goes to sleep, give true dreams of whatever
the mind hath before determined, viz.:—Thou shalt
make an image of the sun, the figure whereof must
be a man sleeping upon the bosom of an angel;
which thou shalt make when Leo ascends, the sun
being in the ninth house in Aries; then write upon
the figure the name of the effect desired, and also
on the hand of the angel.

Let the same image be made in Virgo ascending,
Mercury being fortunate in Aries in the ninth, or
Gemini ascending, Mercury being fortunate in the
ninth house in Aquarius; let him be received by
Saturn with a fortunate aspect, and let the name of

the spirit (Raphael) be written upon it. Let the
same also be made, Libra ascending, Venus being
received from Mercury in Gemini in the ninth house,
and write upon it the name of the angel of Venus
(which is Anael.) Again make the same image,
Aquarius ascending, Saturn fortunately possessing the
ninth in his exaltation, which is Libra, and let there
be written upon it the name of the angel of Saturn
(which is Cassial). The same may be made with
Cancer ascending, the moon being received by
Jupiter and Venus in Pisces, and being fortunately
placed in the ninth house, and write upon it the
spirit of her moon, (which is Gabriel).

There are likewise made rings of dreams of wonderful efficacy, of the sun and Saturn, and the con-
stellation of them is, when the sun or Saturn ascend
in their exaltation in the ninth, and when the moon
is joined to Saturn in the ninth, and in that sign
which was the ninth house of the nativity, and write
and engrave upon the rings the name of the spirit of
the sun or Saturn, and by these rules you may know
how to constitute more yourself. But such images
work nothing (as they are simply images), except
vivified by a spiritual and celestial virtue, chiefly by
the ardent desire of the soul of the operator. But
who can give a soul to an image, or make a stone,
or metal, or clay, or wood, or wax, or paper to live?
Certainly no man whatever; for this arcanum doth
not enter into an artist of a stiff neck. He only
hath it, who transcends the progress of angels, and
comes to the very Arch-type himself. The tables
of numbers likewise confer to the receiving of
oracles, being duly formed under their own constel-
lations.

Therefore he who would receive true oracles by

dreams, let him abstain from supper, drink, and be otherwise well disposed, so that his brain will be free from turbulent vapours ; let him have his bed-chamber fair and clean, let him perfume the same with some fumigation, and anoint his temples, with some unguent efficacious hereunto, and put a ring of dreams upon his finger ; then let him take one of the images we have spoken of, and place the same under his head, and go to sleep, meditating upon that which he desires to know. So shall he receive a most undoubted oracle by a dream, when the moon goes through the sign of the ninth of the revolution of his nativity, and when she is in the ninth sign from the sign of perfection.

INTERPRETATIONS OF DREAMS.

ABUSE. To dream you are insulted and abused, shows you will have some business dispute or other.

ADULTERY.   To dream you have committed it, shows great contentions ; but to dream you have resisted it shows victory over your enemies.

ADVERSARY.   To dream you are in a personal dispute with a person, shows you will meet opposition ; if you draw his blood, you will overcome him, if he draws yours, the contrary, but if neither, you will settle amicably. If you are a lover, and dream you overcome, you will conquer some powerful rival, and be happy.

AIR. To dream you see the air clear, blue, calm, and serene, shows you will attain to what you are aiming at ; if streaked with white, you will get over your difficulties ; but if of thick, dark clouds, disappointments or sickness.

ALTAR. To dream you are at the altar, shows

affliction, and difficulty in getting over it; to dream you receive the sacrament is very unfavourable, and denotes many heavy and severe afflictions.

ANCHOR. This signifies great assurance and certain hope, and success. If you are in love, you must be very persevering to obtain the object of your wishes, or your passion will not meet with success; but beware of a false friend, he professes great attachment but only to deceive you, though all his endeavours to harm you will be in vain.

ANGEL. This is a proof that there is one near you, and that the remainder of your dream will prove true; if you are in love, nothing can be more favourable. If a woman with child dreams of angels, she will have a good time, perhaps twins.

ANGER. To dream of another in a passion with you, denotes very unpleasant circumstances for you; if you seem angry with others, be sure some design is formed to injure you in fortune or reputation.

ANGLING. To dream you are angling, shows affliction and trouble in something you desire.

ANTS. When you dream of ants busy in making their provision, it shows your industry will be crowned with success; if they appear to you as devoured by other animals, or otherwise injured, some secret enemy is at work to compass your ruin; if they are totally destroyed, some fatal reverse is awaiting you; if you are sick, expect a lingering recovery, but moderate exercise, care, and the application of proper means may hasten it.

APES. To dream of apes forebodes no good, but wicked and secret enemies; be on your guard, a deceitful friend is about to deceive you, and you are near losing your liberty; if you are in love, marry not, for he or she will be unfaithful and trouble-some.

APPAREL. If you dream you are genteelly dressed, and in good company, it shows speedy advancement in rank; if your apparel is shabby, you may expect trouble, domestic strife, and loss of goods; if you are dressed in white, you will succeed in the first thing you undertake; if in black, beware of a quarrel, a law-suit, a fit of sickness, the death or elopement of a near friend; if in blue, you will be very happy at an approaching merry-making; if in green, you will shortly go a long journey; if in yellow, you will experience some trouble, very likely the incontinency of the person you have most at heart; if in scarlet, you are in great danger of sickness and heavy crosses; and if you appear in different colours, your life will be somewhat chequered. If you see others in those colours the same things will happen to them.

ARMS. To dream your arms are withered, shows you will decline in health and fortune; if plump and brawny, unexpected prosperity; if broken, you will lose some dear friend by his removing to a great distance from you; if your right arm is cut off, you will lose a near male relation, if the left, a female.

ARMED MEN. If you are pursued by such, and have a difficulty in getting away, you will have some very heavy trouble; if you fight with them, and conquer, your next enterprise will succeed, otherwise you will find this an evil dream.

ASS. To dream of riding on an ass, signifies you will be guilty of some very foolish action, for which you will condemn yourself heartily; if he is feeding, your servants will be diligent and faithful; if you are driving him, you will overcome your trouble ; if he runs after you, some silly person will occasion a laugh against you ; if he appears loaded, you will advance your fortune.

BACK. If your back is broken out in blotches, secret enemies are injuring you ; if you show your naked back, you will be engaged in some scene of lewdness ; if your back is broken, you will suffer loss ; but if it grows stronger, you will receive an unexpected addition to your fortune.

BACON. To dream of bacon denotes the death of a friend or relation, and that enemies will endeavour to do you mischief. In love, it shows disappointment and discontent. Salt beef, ham, and all salt provisions signify the same.

BAGPIPES. To dream of them indicates great trouble, bad success at sea, shipwreck ; in love, that the marriage state will be full of care and poverty.

BAILIFFS. To dream that you are arrested by them, is a sign you will escape a heavy misfortune, that you will not marry your present sweetheart, and that you will be overreached in a bargain.

BALL. To dream you see persons dancing at a ball, or are at a ball yourself, shows joy, recreation.

BANQUET. To dream of banqueting, shows you will be disappointed in an interesting circumstance.

BARLEY BREAD. Eating this, shows health.

BARN. To dream you see a barn well stored with corn, shows you will marry a rich wife, overthrow your adversaries at law, have inheritances, or grow rich by trading, and have good servants ; also banqueting or merry-making. If you dream you see an empty barn, just the contrary.

BASIN. Eating or drinking out of a basin, shows

you will soon be in love, but great care is required, or you will not marry your first lover.

BAT. Not good, except for women with child.

BATHING. This shows hardships; and if in love, to both you and your sweetheart. But if the water be clear, it shows happiness and prosperity in love.

BATTLE. To see a battle in the street, denotes secret enemies, your sweetheart is false ; tumult.

BAY TREE. Success in your undertakings.

BEANS. This dream is unfavourable; the forerunner of trouble and quarrels; and if in love, expect a quarrel with your sweetheart.

BEAR. To dream of a bear, shows vexation and injury from some powerful enemy. The same of a boar, lion, tiger, buffalo, or any other wild animal.

BEARD. To dream of having a bushy beard, indicates you will get all you wish; if it falls off, a speedy decline will ensue. A lady the same.

BEDSIDE. To dream of a maiden's bed-side, or talking with her denotes marriage.

BEER. Signifies enemies.

BEES. If you see bees at work, prosperous industry; if flying about, bad reports of you; if they sting you, loss of goods, reputation, or your lover.

BEHEADING. To dream you see any one beheaded, is a good omen—if in love you will marry the object of your affections; if in prison, you will soon be free; if in trouble, it will soon vanish; and that you will see a friend who has been long absent.

BELLS. To hear bells ringing, brings good news to some, but generally denotes alarm and wrangling, especially if the dreamer is married.

BIRDS. If you see them flying, you will take a

long journey, or hear sudden news; if they seem sportive in their flight, your journey will be pleasant and prosperous; but if they are the contrary, you will have sickness, danger, and losses. If they are perched and singing, it shows a speedy marriage, prosperity, birth of a child, recovery from sickness.

BLEEDING. To dream you see another bleeding, denotes he will endeavour to gain some advantage over you; if you draw the blood, you will gain the advantage over him, and get money from him; but if he draws blood from you, you will lose your suit, whether in law, love, or anything else.

BLIND. To dream you are blind, shows you have placed confidence in one who is your inveterate enemy; avoid errors, particularly in love affairs.

BLIND MAN'S BUFF. To dream you are playing at it, signifies prosperity, joy, and pleasure.

BLOWING THE FIRE. This dream shows anger.

BOAT. To dream you are in a boat on clean water is a good dream, but if you are alone, it denotes that your friends will forsake you; if in danger of drowning, you may expect a strong opposition to your favourite wish; if the boat upsets, renounce your expectations.

BREAD. If you see a great number of loaves denotes success in trade. Eating good bread, you will soon make a valuable acquaintance; but if the bread appears bad, you will lose a friend.

BREWING OR BAKING. This dream shows your servants are knaves.

BRIARS. In your dream, if you are going through briars, you will suffer by enemies; if they make you bleed, your prosperity will be diminished; if you escape without detriment, your foes will persecute you in vain.

BRIDGE. If you are going over a bridge, and meet with no interruption, you will go through life in a prosperous and contented manner; but if you fall down, you will meet an unexpected misfortune.

BULL. To dream you have been gored, or hurt by a bull, shows harm from a lord or some great person; if you receive any good by a bull you will receive it from a lord.

BURIAL. To see a person buried shows you will hear of the death of a relation; if accompanied by one of your family, either he, or one very dear to him will die.

BUYING. To dream of buying victuals raw, denotes benefit from friends; if cooked, you will receive a legacy; if you are buying edge tools, it signifies you will feel a resentment against some one who was before dear to you; if of buying clothes, you will receive some great unexpected benefit.

CAKES. To dream you make one, shows joy and profit; to dream of cakes without cheese, is good; but to dream of both, signifies deceit in love.

CANDLES. This shows you will soon have a quarrel with some person; if the candle goes out, some one of the party will be killed or wounded; if new candles come in, and continue lit, reconciliation.

CAPON. To dream it crows, shows trouble.

CARDS. If you dream you are playing at cards, it shows you will soon be in love. If you hold a many court cards, if you are single, you will soon be married; if many spades amongst them, you will fall into trouble on account of your gratifications in love; if most of them are clubs, you will gain a fortune by marriage; if hearts, you will marry for love, and be very happy; if diamonds, your companion will be of a sour disagreeable temper.

CARROTS. This dream shows prosperity in lawsuits and love affairs; healthy children.

CATS. This dream denotes trouble and vexation to a lover, your sweetheart treacherous; if the cat is plain, smooth, and fair looking, treachery; if it is lean, ugly, without fur, be on your guard, for assassins and robbers await you.

CATTLE. If driving cattle, prosperous undertakings; if they are feeding peaceably, easy fortune; if fighting amongst themselves, you will be chosen umpire in a dispute; if they are bleeding, you will gain by the contests of others.

CHEESE. This dream denotes profit.

CHILDREN. This denotes success. If a woman dreams she is with child, and is not big, she will be; if a man dreams he is *enceinte*, if poor, he will become rich, and if rich, he will be in pain; if a maid so dream, she must be on her guard, or she will lose her virtue. To see children, promises fortune; if handsome, valuable friends; if lean, ragged, and dirty, injury to your reputation; to see them born, shows happiness in your family; to see them die, you will meet with misfortune.

CHURCH. If you are at church, disappointment.

CLOCK. To hear the clock strike, shows your speedy marriage. If it falls, danger to the sick.

COACH. If riding in a coach, prosperity; if a gilt and handsome coach, you will rise in the state; if a hackney coach, a lucrative employment; but if it break down, you will be turned out in disgrace.

COAL PIT. You will marry a widow.

COALS. Riches, discontent, and trouble; burning coals, prosperity, especially in love, where the affections will be mutual, and the union happy; extinguishing coals, loss of life or fortune.

COMBAT. Combating shows enemies; if you get the better of them, good, if they conquer, it is bad.

COMETS. To see a comet is ominous of war, famine, plague, and death; to the lover, frustration of his hopes; to the farmer, failure of his crops; to the seaman, storms and shipwrecks. After such a dream, if possible, change your present abode.

CORN. To see corn fields, or that you are among corn, denotes success in business, joy to the lover; if a sailor, a prosperous voyage; to be gathering ripe corn, promises success in enterprizes; but if it is blighted or mildewed, you will be a considerable loser; if green, it will be a long time before you gain your purpose; but if it becomes suddenly ripe, an unexpected inheritance; you will have an amiable wife, many and happy children, and become rich and happy. To dream of pease and all sorts of grain is good, as they signify abundance.

CROCODILE. This shows a treacherous friend.

CROSS. To see a cross signifies sadness.

CROWNS. This dream shows riches and honour.

CUCUMBERS. This denotes recovery to the sick; you will fall speedily in love; or, if in love, early marriage; and moderate success in trade.

DANCING. Unexpected legacy, and joyful news from a long absent friend. See *Ball*.

DARKNESS. This is a token of affliction and loss; to come out of darkness, rising from obscurity to eminence, escaping from prison or honourably acquitted of a crime you will be accused of.

DEAD. To see a friend who is dead, shows you will hear of a friend who has been long absent.

DEATH. To dream of death, shows a wedding, that yourself is dead, that your present design will succeed, to see and be afraid of the dead, denotes a treacherous friend; if he has a wife, a separation from her, or from friends.

DEBT. To dream you are in debt, pursued by bailiffs, that you will fall into difficulties.

DEVIL. This, without fear, shows you will overcome your enemies; if with fear, some danger; to the tradesman, good business, but many troubles.

DIRT. Dirt denotes sickness and dishonour; to fall into it, treachery and disturbance by some one.

DIVINE SERVICE. The death of a relation.

DOGS. If they fondle with you, you will have sure friends; if you provoke them, you will create yourself enemies; if they bite you, you will suffer loss; if you are in love, be careful of your lover.

DRUNKENNESS. You will find a serviceable friend.

EAGLES. An eagle very high in the air, denotes prosperity, riches, honour; to the lover, success.

EARTHQUAKES. This warns you that your affairs are about to take a very great change.

EATING. This denotes profit; a loathing of victuals, disunion in your family, losses in trade, and disappointments in love; others eating, prosperity.

ECLIPSE OF THE MOON. To see an eclipse, shows the loss of some female friend; your sweetheart is unfaithful; and certain poverty and misery.

EGGS. Eating eggs, shows prosperity; breaking

them, public affront; buying them, good luck; if you sell and get gold, your children will rise to great wealth, if silver, happy in marriage.

ELEPHANTS. Good luck, riches, happy wedlock.

ENEMY. If of fighting with an enemy, a quarrel or a law-suit; if afraid of him, he will get the better of you; if he runs away, you are successful.

ENJOYMENT. This shows speedy marriage.

EVIL SPIRITS. This denotes sickness; if you exercise them, and they vanish, difficulties will vanish.

EXECUTION. An execution, or the place of execution, denotes you will be applied to for relief.

EYES. If you lose your eyes, decay of circumstances, death of a dear friend, disappointment in love; if you get new eyes, or more than you ought to have, shows increase of family.

FACE. That your face is swelled, shows wealth and honour; but if pale, severe disappointment.

FALL. To fall from a high place, and are injured, shows loss; but uninjured, triumph.

FEAST. To dream you are at a feast, denotes extraordinary satisfaction.

FIELDS. If of ploughed fields, unexpected misfortune; if covered with corn, marriage, children, or a legacy; if covered with grass, prosperity.

FINGER. A cut finger, and bleeding, shows you will have a law-suit about money previously paid.

FIRE. To dream of fire, denotes health and happiness; eating fire, shows ruin of health or fortune, and trouble; houses on fire, unpleasant news; in the midst of a fire and feel pain, envy, debates, and displeasure; if that you kindle a fire without trouble, and burns directly, shows that your children will be fortunate;

but if you kindle a fire with much trouble, and it is extinguished presently, it shows dishonour, especially to women ; to see a ship on fire at sea, denotes great loss in business ; to see burning lights descending from heaven, portends dreadful accidents, and to the lover, loss of the affection of your sweetheart, and to the tradesman, bad success in business ; to be burnt, shows danger, and enemies ; and to the sailor, ship-wreck.

FISH. If you are fishing, and catch none, you will court one whom you will never marry ; if you catch any, you will be successful in love ; but if they slip out of your hands, the person you are united to will be of a very lewd disposition, or your best beloved friend will betray you.

FLIES. This shows many enemies and harrassed circumstances ; that your sweetheart cares little for you. To dream you kill flies is very good.

FLOWERS. If gathering flowers, prosperity ; if walking, sitting, or lying on them, marriage and every other happiness ; if they wither in your hands, loss of wife or child, and your happiness.

FOLLY. If a woman dreams she is foolish and guilty of folly, she will have a boy, who will in time grow great ; if a maid, will marry an honest man.

FORTUNE. To make a sudden fortune, is a bad omen ; but to be acquiring one, shows you will inherit one from a rich relation.

FRUIT. Gathering green fruit, denotes sickness ; ripe, mellow, and red, is a token of prosperity.

FUNERAL. That you go to a funeral, denotes a marriage or fortune ; to see a hearse, with a relation attending it, shows that he will lose his nearest friend, who will be related to you.

GALLOWS. To dream of the gallows denotes riches and honours; to the lover the consummation of his wishes, riches and happiness.

GARDEN. If you are walking in a garden, you will be elevated in fortune and dignity; to the lover it denotes success; to the tradesman increase of business; gathering the produce foretells happiness in marriage and good children.

GEESE. These denote the return of an absent friend; success and riches; faithful sweethearts.

GIANTS. To dream of giants is good; if in trade increase of business from foreign parts.

GIFTS. To receive a gift portends sorrow and adversity, and inconstant sweethearts; to give one, joy, and a speedy and happy marriage.

GLASS. Denotes inconstancy and lust; if you crack it, unlawful connection with 'a person who will forsake you.

GLOBE. To dream you are looking at a globe, foretells good, and that you will be a traveller, you will not marry your present sweetheart, but will fall in love and marry in a distant place, become rich, and live happy.

GOLD. If you dream you are receiving gold in bars, you will get an inheritance; if in coin, prosperous affairs; if you pay gold, you will be respected; if you let gold fall, beware of an unexpected attack; if you pick it up you will be reconciled to a person with whom you have quarrelled.

GRAVE. A grave denotes sickness and disappointment; if in love you will never marry your present sweetheart; if you go into the grave, it foretells prosperity; if you take a person out of the grave, you will save the life of some one who will make you happy.

GROVES. To dream you have good land, enclosed with pleasant groves, denotes a virtuous and agreeable wife, who will bear you handsome children.

GUNS. Firing guns or cannons, adversity.

HAIL. A hail-storm presages many sorrows.

HAIR. If you dream that your hair is long and hangs over your shoulders, you will be beloved by a person of quality; if it grow short, or fall off, or be cut, you will lose a friend; if it is burned, your lover will prove false; combing your hair denotes success in love and business. Red hair denotes enemies.

HANGED. If you are to be hanged, you will rise above your present condition.

HILL. To dream that you are climbing a hill, foretells arduous undertakings; coming down easily, prosperity; if pushed down, unexpected misfortunes.

HORSE. To see horses signifies intelligence, black horses, death; white horses, marriage; riding upon a horse, change of place; a fall from a horse, difficulty.

HOUSE. Building houses shows success.

HUNTING. To dream you are hunting a hare, foretells disappointment; hunting the fox, if you kill him you will overcome a secret enemy; a stag-hunt foreshows ambition; if you catch him alive, success; if he dies, bad luck.

ICE. This shows your sweetheart is good-tempered and faithful; to the tradesman, it denotes riches; to the farmer, a good harvest; sliding or skating, some useless pursuit; if the ice break, sickness,

INN. Being in an inn denotes poverty, losses in trade, and bad servants.

INFANTS. Denote trouble; to see them playing, great satisfaction from an unexpected quarter.

IRON. To dream you are hurt with iron denotes that you will receive damage.

KEY. The loss of a key is a sign of displeasure; to give one, marriage; to find or receive one, the birth of a child; to dream of keys shows riches.

KING. Speaking to the king or any of the royal family, is disappointment and difficulties; on the fifteenth night of the moon it is a sign of honour.

KISSING. For a man to dream he kisses a maid, and she vanishes before he accomplishes his desire, denotes that next day he sees a great store of good cheer and yet goes supperless.

KNIFE. Knives indicate lawsuits, poverty, disgrace, strife: to hold a knife in your hand, is a sign of enmity; to stab another with it, quarrels; to stab yourself, some egregious extravagance.

LADDER. Climbing a ladder denotes honour in the state; also a happy union.

LAMB. To see a lamb or kid signifies joy and comfort; to bring one to the slaughter, torment.

LAUREL. A laurel tree is a token of victory or pleasure; if you are married it signifies possessions by your wife; if a woman smells or sees laurel, she shall bear children; if a maid, she will be suddenly married; if a man, it shows prosperity and success.

LEAPING. Leaping over walls or bars foreshows accidents; over drains or ditches, false friends.

LETTERS. To receive letters betokens legacies or presents, and that you have a friend of the opposite sex; to send one, you will do a generous action; writing letters foretells pleasant news.

LICE. Lice indicates sickness and trouble.

LIGHT. To dream that you see a light denotes riches and honour; if it go suddenly out, a downfall.

LIGHTNING. This betokens uneasiness; attended with thunder, a termagant wife, disobedient children.

LINEN. To be dressed in fine linen foretells joyful news; if in chequered, difficulty in your affairs.

LION. To see a lion denotes that you will accumulate riches and marry a woman of great spirit.

LOOKING-GLASS. This denotes vanity, deceitfulness, and much trouble.

MAD. To dream you are mad promises long life, riches, happy marriage, dutiful children; to a farmer, good crops.

MAID. To obtain a maid signifies joy; to force one away, weeping; to kiss one and she vanishes before he accomplishes his desire, disappointment.

MARRIAGE. To dream you are being married and you see the priest, presages sickness; to see no priest, slight illness; to assist at a marriage, good news.

MEAT. Raw meat signifies quarrelling; boiled meat, reconciliation; if you long for meat and get it, success; if not, disappointment.

MILK. To drink milk, promises joy; to sell it, crosses in love, and bad trade; to give it, prosperity, happy marriage; to see it flowing from a woman's breast, happiness; to see beasts drink it, profit.

MONEY. Paying money denotes success, the birth of a child, of the gain of a lawsuit; to receive it, prosperity.

MOON. To dream of the moon, foretells unexpected joy, and success in love; the new moon is good for tradesmen, and lovers; the full moon for handsome women, but not to ugly women.

MOUNTAIN. To see steep, craggy mountains, presages difficulties; to a maid, that she will marry a man who will become rich and great.

MULE. This signifies malice and sickness.

MUSIC. To dream you hear sweet music, denotes happiness; if harsh, a sudden reverse.

NAKED. To dream you are naked, and ashamed, betokens loss of friends, and disappointments; to see a person naked, addition of wealth.

NIGHT. Walking alone at night, signifies disasters; if you are walking in gay company, danger of being robbed; if night falls suddenly on you, you will be in danger of losing your life.

NIGHTINGALE. This pretty bird denotes success, plentiful crops, and a sweet-tempered lover.

NIGHT-MARE. To dream of having the nightmare, signifies that you are ruled by a fool.

NUTS. Gathering nuts signifies loss of time in trifling matters; cracking them, that you will court, or be courted by, a person who will treat you indifferently.

NUISANCE. To dream you are troubled with a nuisance, shows some one is trying to injure you; an old tottering house that you fear will fall on you, signifies that you will acquire an estate, by the determination of a lawsuit; a troublesome neighbour, disagreeable affairs, and vexations; removing a nuisance, prosperity.

OAK. To see a fine oak, implies riches, long life.

OLD PERSON. To dream you are caressed by an old person of the other sex, and enjoy pleasure, denotes prosperity, and success.

OLD WOMAN. To dream that you marry an old woman, success in a coming undertaking.

OLIVE TREE. Gathering olives, denotes peace, delight, and happiness; to beat down olive is good to all but servants.

ONION. Eating onions promises the discovery of a treasure, or lost goods; throwing onions away, a quarrel in your family; getting them, the recovery of a sick person in your family.

ORANGES. Eating oranges implies griefs, &c.

ORCHARD. To dream you are in an orchard, promises inheritances; of ripe fruit, you will get your rights; if it is green, they will be delayed.

ORGAN. Playing an organ, signifies joy; any kind of music betokens good news.

OVEN. To see a hot oven, denotes separation from your family.

OYSTERS. Eating oysters shows prosperity, and marriage with a person who is really a virgin, and she will love you; but if they fall from your hands, you will lose her affections.

PALM. To dream you see or smell palm, signifies abundance, prosperity, and success; if a woman, she will have children; a maid, marriage.

PAPER. Clean paper shows a good character, if dirty or scribbled, an unjust action; if written on good bargains; if folded up, painful contradictions; if neatly folded, you will get your wish.

PATH. Walking in a good path, denotes success

in love; if married, you will obtain your desires; if crooked, it shows very false friends.

PEACOCK. To see a peacock, foretells that you will marry a handsome wife, and attain riches and honour; a woman, she will marry a handsome man, and live in a cot.

PIGEONS. Pigeons or doves indicate a happy partner, contentment, and a large family.

PLAYS. To dream you are at a play, betokens happiness in the marriage state, and success in trade; acting a play, seldom indicates evil.

PIT. Falling into a pit indicates misfortunes; to get out of a pit easily, sudden riches.

PLOUGH. To see a plough at work, shows prosperity; if you hold a plough, respect.

POND. A pond in a dream signifies pregnancy; to see many fishes therein, twins; if they are small, the child will be a girl; if large, a boy.

PRAYING. Praying to God, implies happiness.

PURSE. To find a full purse, indicates prosperity; an empty purse, losses; losing one, death of a friend.

QUARREL. Quarrelling denotes discontent, violent enemies, and a false sweetheart.

QUEEN. To see or converse with a queen, denotes advancement to a post of trust, or marriage with a person in that station.

RACE. To run a race on foot, betokens the defeat of your competitors; if on horseback, disappointment.

RAIN. To see soft rain, denotes success in love; in other respects, trouble and vexation.

RAINBOW. A rainbow, change of situation.

RATS. To dream of being attacked by rats, indicates great misfortunes; if you defeat them you will overcome your enemies; to see them playing, shows reconciliation with your enemies; if they fawn on you, they will beg pardon.

RIDING. Riding in a coach with ease and pleasure, denotes vanity and extravagance.

RING. To dream you have a ring on your finger, foretells a union with the one you love; if it falls off, the loss of your lover, wife, or husband.

RISK. To risk a sum of money by betting, cautions you against a change of situation.

RIVER. To see a river with the water clear and smooth, foreshadows a happy life; if muddy, or yellow, afflictions and trouble; if you are in danger of being borne away by the current, it shows perils, lawsuits, and difficulties.

ROSE. Smelling roses in season, indicates good luck; if not in season, the contrary.

ROAST MEAT. Eating roast meat signifies that you are falling into sin; resist temptation.

SAILING. Sailing in a ship on smooth water, denotes prosperity; on a tempestuous sea, misfortunes; to see agreeable objects, or land in a pleasant situation, happiness in love; to sail in a small boat, and gain the harbour, you will make a rapid fortune.

SHARK. To dream of this fish, foretells the loss of your sweetheart; to the tradesman, ill-luck; to the sailor, tempests.

SHEEP. To see sheep feeding, denotes happiness, and prosperity; to see them scattered, persecution of your children; sheep shearing indicates riches; if you shear them you will wrong your neighbour.

SHIPWRECK. To dream you are shipwrecked, betokens misfortunes, except to those detained by force, then it indicates liberty.

SILVER. Getting or picking up small silver coins, foreshows distress; if shillings, you will receive a small sum; if half-crowns, you will be engaged in some lucrative trade.

SNOW. To see the ground covered with snow, is a favourable dream.

SOLDIERS. To see soldiers drawn up in arms, foreshows persecution; if they are pursuing you, you will be disliked by persons in power.

SPIT. To dream you are turning a spit in a kitchen, indicates misfortunes, losses and poverty.

SHAVING. To dream you are being shaved, denotes a treacherous lover, disappointments; if married, infidelity, and discord; to the tradesman, losses.

SUN. To see the sun, foretells riches, and success in love; to see it rise, good news; to see it set, disagreeable news, to the tradesman, losses; to see it overcast, hardships, troubles, and a great change.

SWEETHEART. If you dream of your absent sweetheart, and she be fairer than usual, she is chaste and constant; if pale and sickly, false.

TEMPEST. This dream shows affliction, losses, trouble; to the poor, repose.

THUNDER. Affliction to the rich, repose to the poor.

TOADS. To see toads, augurs enemies and disappointments; to destroy them is victory.

TOMB. To be erecting a tomb, shows marriages

and births, but to see it fall to ruin, shows sickness and destruction to you and your family.

THIEVES. To fall among thieves, shows loss.

THORNS. Signify grief, care, heaviness.

THOUGHTS. Unsettled thoughts signify joy.

TOOTH. To dream of a tooth falling out, shows the loss of a near relation, and much trouble.

TREASURE. Denotes your exposure to the treachery of a person in whom you confide; if not able to carry it away, the loss of property; to bring it off without difficulty, success in your undertakings.

TREES. Cutting down trees, great losses; climbing them advancement in dignity; to see them in blossom, a happy marriage, and many children; to the tradesman, success in business; to the sailor, pleasant and lucrative voyages.

TRUMPET. To hear the sound, troubles, misfortunes; to the lover, his sweetheart insincere.

VAULTS. To dream of being in vaults, deep cellars, or at the bottom of coal pits, signifies you will match with a widow.

VERMIN. To be covered with vermin, shows sickness; but if you cast them off, deliverance.

VICTUALS. Eating them, shows loss of money

VINEGAR. To drink it, shows sickness.

WALKING. In a dirty place, shows sickness and vexation; to a lover, a bad-tempered and unfaithful sweetheart; to the tradesman, dishonest servants, and loss of goods by fire.

WALL. To be on narrow and weak walls, shows dangerous enterprize; to come down without hurt, or the wall falling, denotes success.

WAR. Signifies trouble and anger to all but soldiers and sailors, and such as live by war.

WASHING. To wash or bathe yourself in baths, riches, and health to the sick; but if with your clothes on, sickness and danger.

WASPS. To be stung by them, shows trouble.

WATER. Drinking it, shows trouble and adversity in trade; to cast off clear water from the stomach, you will lose your place; if the water is dirty, you will meet with afflictions.

WEDDING. To dream of a wedding, portends sickness or death of a near relation, disappointment; for a sick man to marry a maid, signifies death; if to a deformed woman, discontent; to a handsome person, much joy.

WEIGHT. To dream your limbs are heavy when you are pursued, is a sign of falling into affliction.

WELL. If a young man draws clear water out of a well, speedy marriage to a fair maid.

WIFE. A man to dream that he sees his wife married to another, denotes some change of affairs, or else separation; a wife so to dream, shows death.

WINDS. High winds, storms, and showers, you will be crossed in love.

WINE. Drinking wine with an absent friend, shows a speedy meeting; but drinking it alone, you will become a drunkard and be ruined.

WOOD. Carrying wood, trouble and affliction; cutting or chopping wood, an affectionate partner, and obedient children; if walking in a wood, that you will be married more than once.

WOLF. An avaricious, cruel, and bad person

WOOL. Buying or selling wool, denotes prosperity and affluence by means of honest industry.

WOUNDS. To the lover, an affectionate partner; to the tradesman, increase of business and profit; if by an enemy, beware of secret injury.

WRESTLING. This forebodes quarrels, strifes, and contention among your neighbours, enemies, and especially in your own family.

YELLOW. To dream of a yellow colour, denotes to the married woman, trouble from a female, and the loss of her husband's affections. To the lover, he will wed a virgin who will be no comfort to him.

YEW TREE. An indication of the funeral of an aged person, by whose death you will receive some benefit, or protection among his relations.

YOKE. To bear a yoke denotes anger; if a woman she'll obey her husband, rule well her house.

YOUNG. To dream you are young, signifies peace, joy, the accomplishment of your desires.

ZONE. This dream shows trouble and vexation: to the merchant loss of goods; to the lover, unhappiness and disappointment.

THE SILENT LANGUAGE.

THIS art is performed by the twenty-four letters of the alphabet on your hands and fingers, which you must learn, and then spell the words you intend your friend to know. The letters are easily learned and remembered. Most of the letters are upon the left, made with the finger of the right and left hand; with the forefinger of the right hand you point to every letter, but sometimes that and the two next fingers make several letters. The vowels are very easy to remember, they being the tops or ends of your five fingers on the left hand, and the Y is formed in the palm of the hand, as follow :—

The end of the thumb is	A
The end of the fore-finger	E
The end of the middle-finger	I
The end of the ring-finger	O
The end of the little finger	U
The table or palm of the hand	Y
One finger upon the thumb	B
Two fingers upon the left thumb	C
Three fingers upon the left thumb	D
Your two fingers laid together	F
Thump your fists together	G
Stroke the palm of both your hands together ...	H
Your fore-finger upon the left wrist	K
One finger upon the back of the left hand ...	L
Three fingers laid upon the same	M
Two fingers laid upon the same	N
Clinch your left hand or fist	P
Clinch your right hand	Q
Link the little fingers together	R
The back of your hands together	S
The end of the fore-finger to the middle joint of the other fore-finger	T
Two fingers on the little finger of the left hand ...	W
Two fingers across	X
Give two snaps with your fingers	Z

FIGURE HAND.

t	s	a	e	i	o	u	l	m	n	r
19	20	1	2	3	4	5	6	7	8	9

b	c	d	f	g	h	k	p	j	d
10	11	12	13	14	15	16	17	18	21

Which is very easy to understand; for example, suppose I wish to write *Fear God*, it is done thus, 13219

—14421—making a dash thus—between each word, to distinguish one word from another.

SECRET WRITING.

That is, putting one letter in the proper place of another, and thus by changing your letters, it will look like another language. As follows:—

| A | E | I | O | U | Y | T | S | N | R |
| B | C | D | F | G | H | K | L | M | P |

Suppose I wish to write the following words— *Honour the King*. Here I must change the letters in the following manner, viz.

yfmſgp kyc tdmu ;

and thus you may write on any subject either to your friend or lover, and the same remain a secret.

BODILY INDICATIONS.

Strength of body is known by a stiff hair, large bones, firm and robust limbs, short muscular neck, firm and erect, the head broad and high, the forehead short, hard, and peaked, with bristly hair, large feet, rather thick than broad, a harsh, unequal voice, and choleric complexion.

Weakness of body is distinguished by a small ill-proportioned head, narrow shoulders, soft skin, and melancholy complexion.

The Signs of long life are strong teeth, a sanguine temperament, middle size, large deep, and ruddy lines in the hand, large muscles, stooping shoulders, full chest, firm flesh, clear complexion, slow growth, wide ears, and large eyelids.

Short life, inferred from a thick tongue, the appearance of grinders before puberty, thin, straggling, and uneven teeth, confused lines in the hand, of a quick but small growth.

A good Genius may be expected from a thin skin, middle stature, blue bright eyes, fair complexion, straight and pretty strong hair, an affable aspect, the eyebrows joined, moderate in mirth, a cheerful countenance, and the temples a little concave.

A dunce may be known by a swollen neck, plump arms, sides, and loins, a round head, concave behind, a large fleshy forehead, pale eyes, a dull heavy look, small joints, snuffing nostrils, proneness to laughter, little hands, an ill proportioned head, either too big or too little, blubber lips, short fingers, and thick legs.

Fortitude is indicated by a wide mouth, sonorous voice, grave, slow, upright posture, large eyes, open and steadfast, the hair high above the forehead, head much compressed or flattened, the forehead square and high, the extremities large and robust, the neck firm, though not fleshy, a large corpulent chest, and brown complexion.

Boldness is characterised by a prominent mouth, rugged appearance, rough forehead, arched eye-brows, large nostrils and teeth, short neck, great arms, ample chest, square shoulders, and a froward countenance.

Prudence is distinguished by a head flat on the sides, a broad square forehead, a little concave in the middle, a soft voice, a large chest, thin hair, light eyes, either blue, brown, or black, large ears, and an aquiline nose.

A good memory is commonly attached to those persons who are smaller, yet better formed in the upper than the lower parts, not fat, but fleshy, of a fair delicate skin, with the poll of the head uncovered, crooked nose, teeth thick set, large ears, with plenty of cartilage.

A bad memory is observable in persons who are larger in their superior than inferior parts, fleshy, though dry and bald. This is contrary to the opinion of Aristotle, who says, that the superior parts being larger than the inferior, signify a good memory, and *vice versa.*

A good imagination and thoughtful disposition, is distinguished by a large prominent forehead, a fixed and attentive look, slow respiration, and an inclination of the head.

A good sight is enjoyed by persons who have black, thick, straight eye-lashes, large bushy eye-brows, concave eyes, contracted inwards.

Short-sighted people have a stern, earnest look, small short eye-brows, large pupils, prominent eyes.

Sense of hearing, those who possess the same in perfection, have ears well furnished with gristle, well channelled and hairy.

Sense of smelling is most perfect in those who have large noses, descending very near the mouth, neither too moist nor too dry.

A nice faculty of tasting is denoted by a spongy, porous, soft tongue, well moistened with saliva.

Delicacy in the touch belongs to those who have a soft skin, sensible nerves, and nervous sinews, moderately warm and dry.

Irascibility is accompanied by erect posture, clear

skin, solemn voice, open nostrils, moist temples, displaying superficial veins, thick neck, equal use of both hands, quick pace, blood-shot eyes, large, unequal, ill-ranged teeth, and choleric disposition.

Timorousness, by a concave neck, pale colour, weak winking eyes, soft hair, smooth plump breast, shrill tremulous voice, small mouth, thin lips, broad thin hands, and small shambling feet.

Melancholy is denoted by a wrinkled countenance, dejected eyes, meeting eyebrows, slow pace, fixed look, and deliberate respiration.

An amorous disposition may be known by a fair slender face, a redundancy of hair, rough temples, broad forehead, moist shining eyes, wide nostrils, narrow shoulders, hairy hands and arms, and well shaped legs.

Gaiety attends a serene open forehead, rosy agreeable countenance, a sweet musical tone of voice, an agile body, and soft flesh.

Envy appears with a wrinkled forehead, frowning, dejected, and squinting look, a pale melancholy countenance, and a dry rough skin.

Intrepidity often resides in a small body, with red curled hair, ruddy countenance, frowning eyebrows, arched and meeting, eyes blue or yellowish, large mouth, and red lines in the hand.

Gentleness or complacency may be distinguished by a soft and moist palm, frequency of shutting the eyes, soft movement, slow speech, soft, straight, and lightish coloured hair.

Bashfulness, by moist eyes, never wide open, eyebrows frequently lowered, blushing cheeks, moderate pace, slow and submissive speech, bent body, and glowing ears of a purple hue.

Temperance or sobriety, is accompanied with equal respiration, a moderate sized mouth, smooth temples, eyes of an ordinary size, either fair or azure, and a short flat body.

Strength of mind is signified by light curled hair, a small body, shining eyes, but a little depressed, a grave intense voice, bushy beard, large broad back and shoulders.

Pride is known by large eyebrows, a large prominent mouth, a broad chest, slow pace, erected head, shrugging shoulders, staring eyes.

Luxury dwells with a ruddy or pale complexion, downy temples, bald pate, little eyes, thick neck, corpulent body, large nose, thin eyebrows, and hands covered with a kind of down.

Loquacity may be expected from a bushy beard, broad fingers, pointed tongue, eyes of a ruddy hue, large prominent upper lip, and a sharp pointed nose.

Perverseness may be dreaded, when we perceive a high forehead, firm, short, thick, immovable neck, quick speech, immoderate laughter, fiery eyes, and short fleshy hands and fingers.

THE ART OF TELLING FORTUNES

BY TEA OR COFFEE GROUNDS.

POUR the grounds of coffee or tea into a white cup, shake them well about in it, that their particles may cover the surface of the whole cup; then reverse it into the saucer that the superfluous parts may be drained off, and the figures required for fortune telling be formed.

The fortune teller must always bend his thoughts upon him or her who wish to have their fortunes told, and upon their rank and profession, in order to give plausibility to their predictions. It is not to be expected on taking up the cup, that the figures will be accurately represented as they are in the cards, but it is quite sufficient if they bear some resemblance to any of the thirty-two emblems; and the more fertile the fancy shall be of the person who inspects the cup, the more he will see in it.

In other respects, every one who takes a pleasure in this amusement must himself be a judge, under what circumstances he is to make changes in point of time, speaking just as suits, in the present, past, or future; in the same manner, their ingenuity ought to direct when to speak more or less pointedly and determinedly with regard to sex.

The roads, or serpentine lines, indicate ways; if they are covered with clouds, and consequently in the thick, they are infallible marks of many past or future reverses. But if they appear in the clear and serene, are the surest tokens of some fortunate change near at hand; encompassed with many points or dots, they signify an accidental gain of money, likewise long life.

The ring signifies marriage; a letter near, it denotes the initial of the name of the party to be married. If the ring is in the clear, it portends happy and lucrative friendship. Surrounded with clouds, denotes that the party is to use precaution in the friendship he is about to contract, lest he should be insidiously deceived; it is most inauspicious, if the ring appears at the bottom of the cup, as it forebodes separation from the beloved object.

The leaf of clover is a lucky sign. Its different disposition in the cup alone makes the difference; when on the top, it shows that good fortune is not far distant, but it is subject to delay, if in the middle or at the bottom. If clouds surround it, it shows that many disagreeable circumstances attend the good fortune; if clear, it prognosticates undisturbed happiness, as bright as the party wish.

The anchor, the emblem of hope and commerce, implies successful business by water and land, if at the bottom of the cup; if at the top, and in the clear part, constant love and fidelity. In thick and cloudy parts, it denotes love, but tinctured with the inconstancy of the butterfly.

The serpent, always the emblem of falsehood and enmity, is here a sign of an enemy. On the top or in the middle of the cup, it promises to the consulting party triumph over his enemy; but he will not obtain it so easily, if the serpent be in the thick and cloudy part. By the letter which appears near the emblem, the enemy may easily be guessed, as it makes the initial of his name.

The letter. By letters we communicate to our friends either pleasant or unpleasant news, and such is the case here; if this emblem is in the clear part, it denotes the speedy arrival of welcome news; surrounded with dots, it announces the arrival of a considerable remittance of money; but hemmed in by clouds, it is quite the contrary, and forebodes some bad tidings, a loss, or some other sinister accident. If it be in the clear, accompanied by a heart, lovers may expect a letter, which secures to the party the possession of the beloved object; but in the thick, it denotes a refusal.

The coffin, the emblem of death, prognosticates the same thing here, or at least a long and tedious illness, if it be in the thick; in the clear, it denotes long life; in the thick at the top of the cup, it signifies a considerable estate left by some rich relation; in the same manner at the bottom, shows that the deceased is not so nearly related to the consulting party.

The star denotes happiness if in the clear, and at the top of the cup; clouded, or in the thick, it signifies long life, though exposed to various troubles. If dots are about it, it foretells great fortune, wealth, high respectability, honours, &c. Several stars denote good and happy children, but surrounded with dashes, shows that children will cause grief and vexation in old age, and that you ought to prevent it by giving them a good education.

The dog being the emblem of faithfulness or envy, has a two-fold meaning here. At the top, in the clear, it signifies true and faithful friends; but if his image be surrounded with clouds and dashes, it shows that those whom you take for friends, are not to be depended on ; but if the dog be at the bottom of the cup, to dread the effects of extreme envy or jealousy.

The lily. If this emblem be at the top, or in the middle of the cup, it signifies that the consulting party either has, or will have a virtuous spouse ; if it be at the bottom, it denotes quite the reverse. In the clear, the lily betokens long and happy life ; if clouded, or in the thick, it portends trouble and vexation, especially on the part of one's relations.

The cross, be it one or more, predicts adversities ; its position varies, and so do the circumstances. If it be at the top, and in the clear, it shows that the misfortunes of the party will soon end, or that he will easily get over them ; but if it appears in the middle or at the bottom of the thick, expect severe trials. If it appears with dots, either in the clear or the thick, promises a speedy change of one's sorrow.

The clouds. If they be more light than dark, the person will have a good result from wishing ; but, if black, it must be given up. Surrounded with dots, they bring success in trade, and in all undertakings ; but the brighter they are the greater will be the happiness.

The sun, an emblem of the greatest luck and happiness, if in the clear ; but in the thick, it denotes grief ; surrounded by dots and dashes, denotes an alteration will speedily take place.

The moon, in the clear, denotes high honours ; in the dark or thick part, sadness, which, however, will pass without great prejudice ; but if it be at the bottom of the cup, the person will be fortunate on water and land.

Mountain. If it represent only one mountain, it indicates the favour of people of high rank, but several of them, especially in the thick, are signs of powerful enemies; if in the clear, denotes friends in high life, who are endeavouring to promote the consulting party.

Tree. One tree only, if it be in the clear, or thick part, points out lasting good health; several trees denote that your wish will be accomplished. If they are encompassed with dashes, it is a token that your fortune is in its blossom, and will require some time to bring it to maturity. If accompanied with dots, you will make a fortune at a distance, where you will reside.

Child. In the clear part, it bespeaks innocent intercourse between the consulter and another person; in the thick part, excess in love affairs, with great expenses; at the bottom of the cup, the consequences of libidinous amours.

Woman, signifies much joy in general. If in the clear, this emblem has more a favourable signification than in the thick; there it shows a very great happiness, here a great deal of jealousy. If dots surround the image, it explains the lady's fertility, or her wealth. The different positions in the cup, show, at the top, and in the middle, that you will be in love with a virgin, but at the bottom, with a widow.

The pedestrian, denotes a merchant, good business, pleasant news, and recovery of lost things. It also signifies that the consulting party will soon enlist, or get some engagement.

The rider, denotes good news from abroad in money matters, a good situation in a foreign coun-

try, or good prospects. He that doubts his fortune
is promised a lasting one.

The mouse. As this animal lives by stealth, it is
an emblem of theft or robbery; if it is in the clear,
it shows you will get again what you lost in a wonderful manner, but if it appears in the thick, you
must renounce this hope.

The rose, or any other flower, the greatest success
in the arts and sciences; if the consulting party be
married, he will have good children, and all the
fruits to be expected from their good education in
his old age.

The heart, if it be in the clear, signifies future
pleasure. It promises joy at receiving some money,
if surrounded with dots. If a ring or two hearts be
together, it signifies that the party is about to be
married, or betrothed; if a letter be perceptible near
it, it shows the initial of a person's name; if the
letter be in the clear, the party is a virgin; if in the
thick a widow.

Garden or wood, signifies a concourse of people;
in the clear, it indicates good friends, of which it
will consist; in the thick or encompassed with
streaks, it warns the consulting person to be cautious, and not to take for his friends those who profess themselves as such.

Birds in general. In the clear, it signifies that the
troubles with which the person shall have to combat,
will soon be over; in the thick, it is a sign of good
living, and of a successful journey, or voyage, which,
if there are dashes, will be directed to a great distance.

Fish denote successful events by water, if in the

clear, which will either happen to the consulter, or improve the state of his affairs beyond the water. If they are in the thick, the consulter will fish in troubled water, and place his confidence upon that which others have lost before him. Surrounded with dots, denotes that his fate calls him to some distant place.

Lion, or any other ferocious beast. At the top, in the clear, it signifies good luck with people of high rank ; at the bottom, it warns the consulter to shun all such intercourse, as he will find persons who will be envious of his fortune, and not see it with indifference.

Green bush, shows the benevolence and favours of all the consulter's patrons ; it gives some hopes of attaining the honour the consulter wishes for ; without foliage, it is a token of caprice of fortune ; in the clear it announces an unexpected remittance of money.

Worms. At the top, or in the middle of the top, it denotes good luck at gambling, and in marriage ; below, it warns the consulter against rivals in courtship, and against enviers in trade.

House indicates at the top of the cup, blessings and success in the consulter's enterprise ; if the present situation be not of the most favourable, trust that it will soon change for the better. In the middle or below, it cautions the consulter to be vigilant over servants, as vigilance alone will prevent injury.

Scythe, if combined with an hour-glass, denotes imminent dangers of all kinds ; below, it signifies a long and prosperous life.

MISCELLANEOUS.

TO CHOOSE A HUSBAND BY THE HAIR.

Black. Stout and healthful, but apt to be cross and surly; if jet black and smooth, and a large portion, will be fond in his attachment, not addicted to lewdness, make a good husband, and take care of his domestic affairs; but if short and curly, will be of an unsettled temper, given to drinking; somewhat quarrelsome, will show much fondness in beginning his addresses, but will be unfaithful afterwards.

White or fair Hair. Will be of a weak constitution, rather stupid, fond of music, will cut no great figure in the world, moderate in his amorous wishes, but will have some children.

Yellow. Inclinable to jealousy.

Light brown. Neither good nor bad, middling in all respects, rather given to women, but upon the whole a good character.

Dark brown. Sensible and good-humoured, careful, attentive to business, and a good husband.

Very dark brown. Of a robust constitution and of a grave disposition, but good tempered and sensible; fond of his wife, though given to ramble occasionally.

Red. Will be artful, cunning, and deceitful, and much given to wenching; loves a chemise so well, that his wife will have scarce one to her back; but has a good temper.

LUCKY DAYS, ETC.

THE day of the week on which the person was born,

is sure to be the best to begin any business, but not to complete it ; Fridays and Tuesdays are the best for women, Sundays and Mondays for men.

There are three months in a year, in which it is not reckoned good to enter a new house, or sign a lease ; those are April, July and November; neither is the 11th of any month good for such projects.

Let women be careful what they transact in the 31st year of their life, for it is to all females a year of importance, whether married or single ; some great change will await them, or they will be under peril or temptation, have a great loss or great gain, go an unexpected journey, or, something or other remarkable will happen, and dark complexioned women have this fate stronger than others.

LOVE PRESENTS AND WITCHING SPELLS.

TAKE three hairs from your head, roll them up in a small compact form, and anoint them with three drops of blood from the left hand fourth finger, choosing this because the anatomists say a vein goes from that finger to the heart ; wear this in your bosom (taking care that none knows the secret) for nine days and nights ; then inclose the hair in a secret cavity of a ring or a brooch, and present it to your lover. While it is in his possession, it will have the effect of preserving his love, and leading his mind to dwell on you.

A chain or plait of your own hair, mixed with that of a goat, and anointed with nine drops of the essence of amber-gris, will have a similar effect. Flowers will have an effect on your lover's mind ; but the impression will be very transient, and fade with the flowers. If your love should be fortunate, and likewise married to the object of your wishes, never reveal to him the nature of the present you made him; or it may have the effect of turning love into hate.

THE RING AND OLIVE BRANCH.

BUY a ring, resembling a wedding ring, and it is best to begin this charm on the person's birthday. Pay for the ring with some trifling coin, for whatever change is received, must be given to some poor person. Be sure to note what may be said in return, such as *God bless you*, or wishing good fortune, as is usual. When arrived at home, write it down on a sheet of paper, at each of the four corners, and on the middle put the two first letters of your name, your age, and the letters of the planets then reigning as morning and evening stars; get a branch of olive, and fasten the ring on the stalk with a string or thread which has been steeped all day in honey and vinegar, or any composition of opposite qualities, very sweet and very sour; cover your ring and stalk with the written paper carefully wrapped round and round; wear it in your bosom till the ninth hour of the night, then repair to the next church-yard and bury the charm in the grave of a young man who died unmarried; and, while you are so doing repeat the letters of your own christian name three times backwards; return home and keep as quiet as possible, till you go to bed, which must be before eleven; put a light in your chimney, or some safe place; and, before midnight, or just about that time, your future husband will present himself at the feet of the bed, but will presently disappear. If you are not to marry, none will come; and, in that case, if you dream before morning of children, it shows you will have them unmarried ; and if you dream of crowds of men, beware of prostitution.

CUPID'S NOSEGAY.

ON the first night of the new moon in July, take a red rose, a white rose, a yellow flower, a blue one, a sprig of rue and rosemary, and nine blades of long grass ; bind all together with a lock of your own hair ; kill a white pigeon, sprinkle the nosegay with the blood from the heart, and some common salt, wrap the flowers in a white handkerchief, and lay it under your head, on the pillow, when you go to rest, and before morning you will see your fate as clear as if you had your nativity cast by the first astrologer in the kingdom ; not only in respect to love, lovers, or marriage, but in the other most important affairs of life ; storms in this dream, foretells great trouble, &c.

ON MAGIC.

THE following very curious narrative is inserted as related by a nobleman of unimpeached veracity ; he said, he went with the Duke of Courland, Prince Albert, of Saxe, and other persons of distinction, to a reputed magician to witness his extraordinary power ; the man took three days for preparation. As they approached the house, they felt an unusual agitation and mental dissatisfaction. Upon entering the great hall, many of the company wept, and their hair stood up, while some experienced violent palpitations of the heart, and were filled with indescribable horror.

After they had composed themselves, the magician led them into a long gallery, on the white walls of which, various figures were visible ; some raving in agony, and some wrapped in ecstacy. The Duke of

Courland asked him if he could raise the shades of particular persons; and answering in the affirmative, there were raised Maria Theresa, Charles XII. of Sweden, Charles I. of England, Henry IV. of France, Voltaire, and Newton, with whom they had an interesting conversation, which they were bound not to divulge. As they were going, Prince Albert wished to see Marshal Saxe; the magician raised him by fresh incantations.

He appeared in the midst of thunder, and looking most horrible, exclaimed—"Wretch, thou hast exceeded thy power, and repent what thou hast done!" However, by the magician's desire, they joined in fervent prayer, and tranquillity was restored.

LOVE'S CORDIAL, TO BE TRIED THE THIRD NIGHT OF A NEW MOON.

TAKE brandy, rum, gin, wine, and the oil of amber, of each a tea-spoonful, a table-spoonful of cream, and three of spring water; drink it as you get into bed, repeating—

> This mixture of love I take for my potion,
> That I of my destiny may have a notion,
> Cupid befriend me, new moon be kind,
> And show unto me the fate that's design'd.

You will dream of drink, and according to the quality or manner of it being presented, you may tell the condition to which you may rise or fall by marriage. Water is poverty; if you dream of a drunken man, it is ominous that you will have a drunken mate. If you dream of drinking too much, you may fall into that sad error yourself.

NEW WAY OF TELLING FORTUNES BY CARDS.

TAKE out of the pack all the cards under seven, only reserve the aces, as these are called the poiuts, and are of most particular consequence; then take out the eights, for they are cards of no meaning; you will then have twenty-eight left, which you must thus manage: shuffle them well, and deal them into four equal parcels; having first decided of what suit you will be the queen, and you must make your lover, or husband, of the same suit as yourself without regard to his complexion; take up the parcel dealt exactly before you, and then proceed regularly round to the right, examining them separately as you proceed. The first tells what is to happen soon, the second at some distance, and the third respects your husband or lover, and the fourth your secret wishes, and you must judge by the cards as to your success.

COURT CARDS.

A number of court cards is good, it tells a meeting or company—if diamonds lay next to them it is mirth—hearts, a wedding or christening—clubs, business—and spades, a funeral—a king and queen singly together, a courtship or wedding—a queen and knave, intrigue—and if spades are near them, the result will be disgrace, and food for scandal—the knaves together, treachery or a suit at law—but the knave of hearts stands for Cupid, and you must find out his errand by the cards round him.

Tens. Shows changes; diamonds, unexpected luck; hearts, a removal; spades, death or a strange bed, according to the next cards; clubs, a new way of life; three or four tens, a very great surprise; two together a visit into the country.

Nines. The nine of spades is the worst harbinger of misfortune in the whole pack, it foretells great evil; the nine of clubs is good for married women, but to single ones, it tells what is usually called a love child: nine of diamonds is good for traders, and the nine of hearts for lovers and widows; they tell changes.

Sevens. Ill luck. The seven of clubs in the pack with yourself, shows a drunken husband; hearts, perfidy in love; diamonds, losses; spades, scandal; three sevens together, an accident; two, imprisonment; four, danger.

The Aces. These vary their meaning according to their situation, turned up singly on the pack. In cutting the cards, the ace of hearts is a rich lover—in the same pack with yourself a house, if not a ship —ace of diamonds, on the pack, a ring; with yourself, a present—in any other pack or parcel, a sum of money; club is always a busy ace, telling news, letters, or new work—let it be placed as it may.

The ace of spades turned up, is an unlucky prognostic—with another spade, death—with clubs, a loss in trade—with diamonds, loss of money—with hearts, unhappy marriage. The four aces together, a good settlement—three, a pleasing surprise—and two an unpleasant one. The ace of diamonds and ten of hearts together, betoken marriage—and in the pack, that betokens your secret wishes, to have either of the tens or aces, or the nine of hearts, tells success, and that your desires will be speedily accomplished.

HELIOGABULUS'S MAGIC TABLETS.

RULE.—Place the little finger on any letter by chance, in the first tablet (it is better to do it with the eyes shut)—then refer to the second tablet, to the letter under which is a magical figure, referring to the oracle in the two following pages, which determines the fortune of the inquirer.

TABLET No. I.

```
        A   C   D
      Z   F   X   L
    N   A   P   N   O   C
  D   L   Q   Y   R   S   T
  E   H   G   L   K   V   W
T   S   V   A   N   M   C   D
P   O   R   B   W   X   A
C   H   C   I   X   F   G   S
  B   H   L   L   W   V   U
  O   F   T   S   V   D   L
      M   X   Z   A   B
    W   B   B   L   M
      O   N   Q   S   Y
```

TABLET No. II.

	A	B	C	
	25	15	5	
D	E	F	H	G
14	16	6	13	7
I	K	L	M	N
18	8	17	1	9
O	P	Q	R	S
10	22	3	12	23
	T	V	U	W
	19	2	24	4
	X	Y	Z	
	20	21	11	

ORACLES TO THE MAGIC TABLETS.

GOOD FORTUNE.

1. If this number is fixed upon by a man, it insures him, if single, a homely wife, but rich; if married an access of riches, numerous children and an old age. To a lady, the faithfulness of her lover, and a speedy marriage.

3. Very good fortune, sudden prosperity, great respect from high personages, and a letter bringing important news.

7. This number, to a single woman, shows a handsome, rich, and constant husband; if married, a faithful partner, of a good family, as she must know she has married above her condition; to a man the same.

8. This is a general good sign, and your present expectations will be fulfilled, and you have some on the anvil.

9. If a married man or woman draws this, if under fifty, let them not despair of a young family; to the single, very sudden marriage.

10. A friend has crossed the sea, and will bring home some riches, by which the parties will be much benefited.

12. An uncommon number belonging to scriptural signs, and shows the party will have success in all their undertakings.

15. No doubt but the chooser is very poor, and thought insignificant, but let friends assist him or her, as they are much favoured.

16. A very sudden journey, with a pleasant fellow-traveller, and the result of the journey will be generally beneficial to your family.

18. A sudden acquaintance with the opposite sex, but which will be opposed; notwithstanding, the party should persevere, as it will be to his or her advantage.

21. A letter of importance will arrive, announcing the death of a relation whom you do not respect, but who has left you a legacy.

22. Be very prudent in your conduct, as this number is very precarious, and much depends upon yourself; it is generally good.

23. A very accomplished young woman will be the wife of the man who chooses this figure.

24. Let the chooser of this number persevere; all his or her schemes are good, and must succeed.

BAD FORTUNE.

2. Shows the loss of a friend, bad success at law, loss of money, unfaithfulness of lovers, and a bad partner.

4. A letter announcing loss of money.

5. The man who draws this number, let him examine his moles, and he will find, I know more about him than he imagines.

6. Very bad success; you may expect not to succeed in any of your undertakings.

11. I should rather suspect the fidelity of your husband or wife, if married; if single, you are shockingly deceived.

13. You want to borrow money, and hope you shall have it, but you will be deceived.

14. The old man you have depended upon is going to be married, and will have a child.

17. You have mixed with this company, and pretend to despise our tablets, but rely much upon them, and you may depend on it that you will be brought to disgrace.

19. Look well to those who owe you money, if ever so little; a letter of abuse may be expected.

20. A drunken partner, bad success in trade, but the party will never be very poor, though always unhappy.

25. The man or woman who chooses this unlucky number, let them look well to their conduct; justice, though slow, is sure to overtake the wicked.

SIBLY'S MAGIC TABLET.

☞ Close your eyes, and place the point of a pin on the following table of Figures, repeating to yourself:—"*Guide my hand, O my ruling Planet!*" Then look for the corresponding figures in "Character of your future Husband, or Wife."

46	53	22	19	41	54	31	12	24
50	64	45	15	10	47	61	20	
14	38	16	27	18	51	21	32	23
4	6	48	25	29	7	17	28	
9	30	3	43	40	55	2	33	39
56	36	8	44	37	57	35	58	
34	1	26	58	49	52	60	5	68
42	67	62	67	59	65	70	63	
13	66	11	60	71	69			

CHARACTER OF YOUR FUTURE HUSBAND.

1 Tall and handsome.
2 Remarkably fat and clumsy, a great load.
3 A great eater.
4 Very amiable in temper.
5 Rather lustful.
6 Very penurious.
7 A real gentleman.
8 A great skin-flint.
9 One who will idolize you.
10 A wealthy man.
11 One who will kiss you to the tune of 13 to the dozen.
12 One given to wenching.
13 A soft imbecile.
14 Rather deformed in the legs.
15 A good moral man.
16 A clerical gentleman.
17 A great sot.
18 A beautiful man, and good.
19 A benevolent person, who will love you.
20 A quack doctor.
21 One who will love you through life.
22 A hump back or "mountain in misery."
23 A clever and worthy trades-man.
24 A man of fine taste.
25 A person of low occupation.
26 A man kind, indulgent.
27 One who will incessantly love you, day and night.
28 Would be handsome if he did not squint.
29 Florid complexion, beautiful eyes.
30 A merchant — a dignified figure.
31 A warm-hearted sailor.
32 A good fellow, but lost his teeth.
33 So good that all will envy you.
34 A military character.

35 One whom you will have to nurse.
36 One whose passions are very frigid — *no steam there.*
37 A very pious character.
38 A great sloven, fond of his glass.
39 One whom you may govern.
40 A man who will keep his purse closed.
41 A cross, waspish fellow.
42 Bald and venerable.
43 One with a brilliant genius.
44 A beardless boy, whom you will have to curb.
45 One fond of literature.
46 Very tall, and small as a whipping post.
47 A stale Bachelor, who has long wanted a mate.
48 One always refused.
49 A loving and faithful man.
50 One with a painted face.
51 A sweet husband and loving father.
52 One who will study your interest at all times.
53 A widower with three fine girls, and four rough boys, with a moderate income.
54 A young boy, with very precocious talent for wedlock.
55 A man of commanding influence.
56 A widower with grey hair.
57 A good honest soul, very fatherly.
58 One who will ardently love you during honeymoon, but wither away afterwards.
59 A merry-andrew.
60 A country bumpkin.
61 A man worth nothing.
62 A common spendthrift.
63 A good husband.

64 A clandestine marriage with a horse jockey.
65 A petty-fogging lawyer.
66 A traveller.
67 One universally admired.
68 One who will do good to all around him.
69 A dutiful husband, but very simple.
70 A precise quaker.
71 Will weep if you chide him.

CHARACTER OF YOUR FUTURE WIFE.

1 A lady of good birth
2 One rather advanced in years, who will be very motherly to you.
3 Very handsome, but rather deaf.
4 A fine rosy girl.
5 A buxom widow.
6 One rejected by all but yourself.
7 An accomplished female.
8 A robust vulgar lass.
9 A high spirited dame.
10 Good lady, but bow-legged.
11 A model of goodness.
12 O that sweet face, and amiable mind.
13 A real termagant, who will now and then *bate* you.
14 A good partner, ever willing to be guided by you.
15 A good nurse, whom you will require.
16 One who will always have the last word.
17 Affable and kind, a soother in sorrow.
18 Mrs. Caudle, an able Curtain Lecturer.
19 A regular scold.
20 Amiable and sympathetic.
21 A fruitful vine, 13 as 12.
22 Contour of the countenance good, but the eyes odd.
23 Quality pretty good, but quantity very limited.
24 Has trifled with all her suitors and at last taken to you.
25 Twins every 2½ years.
26 Very extravagant, and will defy you.
27 One who will strive to please you.
28 A very pious lady.
29 One who ought to be boarded at a Drapers' Shop.
30 One very intellectual.
31 A real Dorcas, loving charitable deeds.
32 The Lady will patronize Gin.
33 Very economical, and to be trusted.
34 One who will run you into debt.
35 Would be handsome, if the squint was not so extremely bad, looking three ways at once.
36 Very pretty, but likely to have a beard.
37 Very modest and neat.
38 One who has a gray hair here and there, snows of age approximating.
39 A real gossip—not keeping at home.
40 A help-mate for you in every respect.
41 Fond of having parties, and going to parties.
42 A good wife, an affectionate mother.
43 You will have to dwell in sterile regions.
44 A bad wife and bad children.
45 She will love you in adversity as well as in prosperity

46 You will ardently love her—beautiful children.
47 One young enough to be your daughter.
48 High in wisdom, sweet in converse.
49 A lady of fortune, not haughty.
50 Old enough to be your mother.
51 Will always esteem you.
52 You will be a cuckold.
53 Slovenly and dirty.
54 A scold, bad tempered.
55 An angel in disguise.

56 She will desert you and your large family.
57 You will always love her.
58 A Fury!—woe be to you.
59 A ministering angel
60 Fat and ugly.
61 A good wife.
62 Altogether unmanageable.
63 A quakeress.
64 A regular dolly.
65 An authoress.
66 One from a foreign land.
67 Your housemaid.
68 A black woman.
69 One too many for you.
70 A real christian.